The Australian Résumé Guide
Making Your Job Application Work

The Australian Résumé Guide
Making Your Job Application Work

Including

Web Sites for Job Seekers

PAUL STEVENS

The Centre for Worklife Counselling
Sydney

COPYRIGHT

Copyright laws protect the rights of creators, including authors and publishers. They provide a valuable incentive for such creators to produce current and relevant information.

Please respect copyright. Abuse of copyright through any means, including photocopying increases the price of educational materials. Without copyright protection, authors would be deprived of income and fewer titles would be available.

This book is copyright. Except as permitted under the Copyright Act 1968, for example any fair dealing for the purpose of private study, research, criticism or review, no part of this book may be reproduced, stored in a retrieval system, or transmitted in any form or by any means without prior written permission. All inquiries should be made to The Centre for Worklife Counselling at the address below.

Copying for educational purposes

The Copyright Act 1968 allows a maximum of one chapter or 10% of this book, whichever is the greater, to be copied by any educational institution for its educational purpose provided that that educational institution has given a remuneration notice to the Copyright Agency Limited ('CAL') under the Copyright Act 1968 or there is a licence agreement between CAL and that educational institution or the body that administers that educational institution (e.g. Department of Education).

In the absence of such an agreement or remuneration notice, an educational institution must seek written permission for any copying from the copyright owner, or its exclusive licensee, and make payment, if requested. All inquiries should be made to The Centre for Worklife Counselling at the address below.

For details of the CAL licence for educational institutions or which educational institutions can give CAL a remuneration notice, contact CAL, Level 19, 157 Liverpool Street, Sydney NSW 2000. Tel: (02) 9394 7600 Fax: (02) 9394 7601 Email: info@copyright.com.au

Published in Australia by
The Centre for Worklife Counselling (Established in 1979)
Suite 3, 5 Earl Street, (PO Box 407, Spit Junction 2088) Mosman NSW 2088, Australia
Tel: (02) 9968.1588   Fax: (02) 9968.1655
Email: worklife@ozemail.com.au   Website: www.ozemail.com.au/~worklife

First edition, 1990
Second edition, 1998

© Worklife Pty Ltd 1998

Stevens, Paul, 1941-.
    The Australian résumé guide : making your job application work including web sites for job seekers.

Includes index.
ISBN 1 875134 37 9

1. Résumés (Employment). 2. Applications for positions. 3. Job hunting - Australia - Directories. I. Centre for Worklife Counselling (Sydney, NSW). II Title.

650.14

Editing and design by Ann Reynolds

Contents

About the Author

Paul Stevens founded The Centre for Worklife Counselling in Sydney in 1979 following a 21 year career in Personnel Management and The Worklife Network— a national and international affiliation of adult career specialists—in 1986. He wrote his first published contribution to adult career development in 1981, *Win That Job!*, closely followed by *Stop Postponing the Rest of Your Life*. Over 30 further titles, booklets and career assessment instruments have been published since, the latest being *A Passion for Work: Our Lifelong Affair* and *Separation and Outplacement: Managing Both Effectively*.

Paul's dedication to assisting adults in transition has been recognised in many ways—he is Fellow of the Australian Association of Career Counsellors, Visiting Fellow in Adult Career Development, University of Wollongong; International Board for Career Management Certification (IBCMC); Member, Board of Directors, International Career Planning & Adult Development Network; Fellow Practitioner and Member, Board of Governors, International Association of Career Management Professionals; Member, Editorial Board, Career Development International Journal (MCB Press); and Co-Founder of the Australian Human Resources Institute (AHRI) Career Development Special Interest Group.

Other books and career assessment instruments by Paul Stevens

Career Action Constraints Card Sort Kit
Career Development Support in Organisations
Career Management: Whose Responsibility?
Handling Office Politics
Helping Your Child Choose a Career
How to Network & Select a Mentor
My Career, My Life, Myself
Occupational Work Settings Card Sort Kit
A Passion for Work: Our Lifelong Affair
Planning For Me! Setting Personal Goals
Résumé Training Kit
Separation and Outplacement: Managing Both Effectively
Stop Postponing the Rest of Your Life
Strategies for Dual-Career Couples
Win That Job!

About this Guide

This Guide is a workbook designed to help you apply for jobs in the most effective way. The aim of *The Australian Résumé Guide* is to help you to develop a job application that will show an employer or employment agency consultant the benefits of hiring you and result in an interview invitation to discuss your employment. The Guide will also help the reader who is preparing an internal job application within their current employment environment.

The Guide gives well-proven advice and shows methods of presentation to make sure that you produce the best possible job application. It provides details on how to construct a résumé (pronounced 'rez-yoo-may'). It also shows you how to create the other essential part of your job application—the letter which accompanies your résumé. There are also hints on writing, designing, typing and printing your letter and résumé. These will help you make sure that your final job application presentation is appealing to the reader both visually and in content.

The Guide includes samples drawn from a wide range of occupations, and checklists to help you construct your own drafts and ensure you include everything that is required.

It is important that you read most of the résumé samples, not just those relevant to your employment objective. The reason is that the résumés illustrate solutions to many awkward career record problems, such as:

- too many past jobs;
- returning to workforce after a long absence;
- background of multiple careers.

The sample résumés are arranged into sections for:

- job seekers who are wanting to or have to change employers (pages 27-158);
- those who are currently concluding their secondary or tertiary education (pages 188-201).

Similarly, there are sections containing sample job application letters for:

- job seekers who are wanting to or have to change employers (pages 170-177);
- those who are currently concluding their secondary or tertiary education (pages 202-207).

Another section provides advice, checklists and samples to help you write follow-up letters ranging from interview follow-up to accepting an offer of employment (pages 178-183).

If you believe you need a competent adviser for your career transition, I've included recommendations for selecting a career counsellor (pages 211-212).

I am confident that the contents of *The Australian Résumé Guide* will contribute to your success. The techniques have been developed while the company I founded, The Centre for Worklife Counselling, has helped people in transition since 1979. I believe that this Guide will help make your job applications successful. I am confident that if you pay close attention to all the recommendations, you will discover a great many good points about yourself and your background which will help you develop your self-confidence in the difficult process of getting a worthwhile job.

Paul Stevens
Fellow, Australian Association of Career Counsellors
Mosman, Sydney 1998

Preparation for Job Hunting

✓

Yes/No

- I have identified my assets in terms of skills, abilities and past achievements ❑ ❑

- I have identified my preferences for using my skills ❑ ❑

- I have thought about and defined my preferred work-life-style ❑ ❑

- I have written notes which summarise my experience in terms of work, education and vocational activities ❑ ❑

- I have identified personality characteristics that should be considered in selecting my next boss ❑ ❑

- I know my feelings about the work environment setting I would like ❑ ❑

- I have researched at least two career path possibilities ❑ ❑

- I have talked to one or more people in the field I am targeting ❑ ❑

- I have identified the relevant actual job titles I am considering ❑ ❑

- I have identified employers or people relevant to my career path choice ❑ ❑

- I have an understanding of the different approaches used to obtain interviews ❑ ❑

- I have identified additional skills-building needs I should acquire in my next job ❑ ❑

- I have obtained past employer references ❑ ❑

- I have studied the interview process through relevant books, audio tapes and/or have had discussions with a career counsellor ❑ ❑

- I have identified sources of career transition help I might need ❑ ❑

- I have reasonable alternatives in mind if unable initially to get my first choice ❑ ❑

- I have talked over my best alternatives with significant others in my life ❑ ❑

If you have ticked more than three 'No', you are not yet ready to go job hunting. Please read the advice on pages 211-212.

The Effective Résumé Writer's Beliefs

✓ My first responsibility is to be true to myself—everything I do is a choice.

✓ It's OK to be apprehensive about change.

✓ I am most likely to be effective for both my employer's benefit and my own, if I focus on a job role and career direction that fit my values and preferred skills.

✓ I will welcome mistakes as opportunities for learning and improving.

✓ No career action step will be resolved without deep consideration of the factors affecting my life outside work.

✓ I will present a résumé which targets activities and responsibilities I would prefer to have more of in my future work.

✓ While I will decide on a specific a career action step, I will remain open for job-seeking target adjustment and unexpected opportunities.

✓ I will weather my job change well by having a safety net of awareness of my preferred skills, career values, primary wants and contribution value to my employer's customers.

✓ I will not be able to achieve my career goals alone and will actively seek the support of others.

✓ The meaning of success for me will alter as I journey through my life—I will take care to redefine it for myself at regular intervals.

✓ I can only promote myself to employers effectively when I know myself and what I want.

1 Preparing Your Résumé

The Importance of Your Résumé

If you put all your information in one long job application letter, you lessen your chances of being chosen for an interview over other applicants. Sending a résumé with a short covering letter is the best approach. It will, however, take more than one attempt to get it right. Most people need to write several drafts before they achieve the best possible result.

It's hard work writing your résumé, but it's a very important part of your job seeking. If it's well arranged, the résumé will serve as a clear statement of your value to a prospective employer.

Your résumé should contain all the details necessary for applying for any job you want in your chosen occupation. During your search you are likely to be applying for many. A covering letter is then used to highlight the parts of your résumé most relevant to each particular vacancy.

You must be prepared to apply considerable effort to make information about yourself easy to understand. Any obstacle to comprehension is likely to lose you invitations for interview. It is not the reader's job to interpret what you are conveying. Your words should communicate plainly so that no interpretation is required.

Career Self-Reliant Behaviour

Yes, a new term is becoming widespread within employment environments. It's about always being alert to ensuring your employability, not for next year or thereafter but for next month. It's about making sure that you have a set of skills and new learning that are relevant to the business needs of your employer. This requires a regular audit of your competencies and the objectives of the work-in-progress around the job role you are targeting.

Career self-reliant behaviour also requires that you know and practise much more than you used to need to know about personal career management. You are expected to initiate proposals for work assignments, desired new learning, transfers, promotions, etc. not wait until they are offered as was the case in the past. Knowledge and skill in personal career management techniques is the new version of job security.

One of these techniques is the ability to communicate to others what you seek and why you merit it. More often than not this is conveyed in the form of a résumé. These used to be only for job seeking outside your employment environment, but today a good résumé is essential to support your case for consideration for a personal career action step when and where you are employed.

This Guide is designed to help you with these career self-reliant behaviours in the production of a résumé which you must keep updated to be always alert to increasing your employability.

Your Value to Employers

Each person can find examples from their past which will show different qualities to employers. When you are preparing a job application, it is not the time to be modest. Tell the reader what you have done in a positive manner. You should include examples in your résumé of your achievements and capabilities stated in such a way that they relate to the job role for which you are applying. This shows you have transferable skills from your past to your new career goal.

Benefits of Your Résumé

Preparing your résumé before you write your job application letter gives you a clear and orderly picture of your talents and your qualifications for employment. Your covering letter allows the employer to get more of an idea of the sort of person you are through the way you write. If the employer is impressed by your letter, it is more likely that your résumé will be read with care.

Your résumé will help to give you a much better chance of being invited for an interview. The time you spend and the thinking involved in preparing it will also help you in face-to-face discussions with prospective employers. Interviewers tend to ask questions based on your written application. After you have worked hard preparing it, you will be able to speak confidently about the contents.

A well-organised job application often sells you as a strong candidate even before an interview. Frequently, this results in fewer questions for you to answer and leaves more time during the interview for you to ask questions and learn whether the job on offer is what you really want.

The Résumé Writing Journey

Look at the process of achieving a new job with the help of your résumé as being a journey with clear steps to be taken in a particular sequence to produce your desired result—arriving at the destination called success!

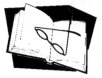

Locate, acquire and read at least three books about making career transitions.

You may think that people you know know all about you, but they don't. Your résumé is an opportunity to educate others about you—relatives, friends, members of your network, people who can introduce you to job opportunities.

Before you start your résumé, seek printed resources or people to help you assess who you really are today and what you want from your worklife.

Carry out several information gathering interviews about the area of work you have in mind.

Check whether the demands of the job you are targeting will allow you time to pursue the other interests in your life.

Plan for at least a week and several re-writes before your résumé will be ready.

Remember you are competing with others with your résumé. It's worth an effort to produce the best version you can.

 Seek the opinions of others about your merits for what you have in mind.

 If you are too modest in describing your attributes, your application may be passed over. It's the time to boast politely and honestly.

 Ask at least two people to check over your final draft using the Checklist on page 23.

 When you think you have produced the best version, be patient. Sleep on it. Read it again the next day before submitting it.

 Keep a diary of the job applications you have made and their progress.

Preparing a Résumé

When seeking a job, your first task is to work out what skills are demanded and what skills you have and want to offer. You can then set them out in a convincing way which will appeal to prospective employers.

Most employers, on average, spend less than one minute on their first reading of a job application. That's a frightening thought: your carefully written résumé and letter will be skimmed through in less than 60 seconds! So it is up to you to capture their interest in that time. Once they are interested, they will read it more thoroughly.

How you arrange the information about yourself is important. Think about some of the printed advertisements that have gained your attention. The advertiser puts a lot of time and effort into the wording and design of advertisements when trying to sell a product or service. Your task is the same—except that you are the product you are trying to promote. You need to be seen as more appealing than other applicants.

Checking Your Target Job Choice

Before you start compiling your résumé, check thoroughly that the information you have gathered matches what you *really* want.

Preferences

Does your target job match your work content preferences? If not, your motivation and productivity will be low.

Yes/No
❑ ❑

New Learning

Are you capable of—and interested in—the new learning on offer?

Yes/No
❑ ❑

Satisfaction

Will the work content satisfy your primary wants for income, environment type, nature of work and the industry?

Yes/No
❑ ❑

Practicality

Do you have a good chance of obtaining the job and have you researched sufficiently to know this?

Yes/No
❑ ❑

Willingness

Are you willing to 'go for it' with thoroughness in your application?

Yes/No
❑ ❑

If you have marked any 'noes', you need to re-evaluate whether going for this job is truly in your best interests.

Beginning the First Draft

When you begin the first draft of your résumé, keep in mind that you need to write clearly and to the point and use correct expression and spelling. If in doubt, ask for advice from someone who, in your opinion, writes well. If necessary, refer to a dictionary.

The people who are going to read your résumé will ask themselves three main questions: Who is this applicant? What sort of job role does this person want? What abilities or skills is this person offering?

Keep your résumé brief—it's best if your finished (typed) version is no longer than two pages, maximum three. Additional information about your career record can be taken to the interview and handed over then. There is, however, no set rule regarding the length of résumés. The discipline of striving for a two page résumé is useful as it encourages you to record only pertinent information and not data which has little or no value towards securing an interview invitation.

Highlight your best points and arrange the information so that you make a good impression in a short reading time. When designing the first page, place your name in the centre at the top. You will be helping the employer to contact you more easily if you place your telephone number prominently on your résumé—i.e. at the top, below your name.

You should include your personal information (address, etc.) in your résumé. Even though your address will also be on your covering letter, make sure you repeat it in your résumé. This is important, because the letter and the résumé may become separated and mixed up with other papers in the employer's offices.

If you choose to include your age, use your date of birth rather than your age, then you will not have to revise your résumé after each birthday!

Don't waste space. For instance, there is no need to put the State in your address if you give the postcode. If you have a temporary address include it, as well as your permanent home address. Another thing, it is better to supply the address of the place where you live rather than to give a post office box number.

Your Career Objective

The first section of your résumé (beneath your name) should comprise a sentence that outlines your career objective. Many find this the hardest section to write. Several attempts may be required before you are satisfied with the result.

If you are uncertain about your career goals, I have written and published two books which will help you. They are *A Passion for Work: Our Lifelong Affair* and *Stop Postponing the Rest of Your Life: Achieving Career Satisfaction*. There is also a workbook available, *My Career, My Life, Myself*, which is designed to help those who are preparing for an internal job application where they work.

Use of Section Headings

Your résumé should be arranged into sections. Often applicants do not give these section headings or their sequence much thought, yet they are a really good way of making your résumé stand out from others. If the section heading is interesting, then the reader is likely to pay more attention to the information in that section.

The use of interesting headings is not the only way you can draw attention to the content of each section. You can put the headings in capital letters, use bold print, centre them above each section or put them to the left of the section data in a wide margin. Here are a range of section headings from which to make your initial selection. The column headings have been numbered 1—9 to show the order in which they should appear in your résumé.

1. Goal
Career Objective
Employment Objective
Career Goal
Employment Aspirations

2. Summary
Key Areas of Knowledge
Special Skills
Main Capability Areas
Précis of Major Skills
Special Areas of Expertise

3. Qualifications
Study Accomplishments
Comprehensive Business-Oriented Education
Educational Preparation for Career
Tertiary Education Achievements
Educational Attainments
Relevant Training and Education
Formal Training
Successful Tertiary Studies
Formal Qualifications

4. Achievements
Career Achievement Summary
Special Achievements
Highlights of My Career
Breadth of Experience
Special Challenges
Précis of Key Projects
Professional Achievement Record

5. Employment	Professional Experience
	Record of Respected Employers
	Career Path Record
	Employment Summary
	Progressive Employment Record
	Employment Record
6. Other Facts About Me	Community Service
	Professional Association Memberships
	Language Knowledge
	Professional Affiliations
7. Personal Development Activities	Special Awards and/or Recognition
	Knowledge Enhancement
	Career Development Learning Experiences
	Self-Development Activities
8. Referees	Referees
	People Who Know Me Well
	People Who Know My Work Well
9. Personal	Personal Information
	Personal Data
	More Facts About Me

List Your Achievements

The main part of your résumé should be made up of brief statements that describe your achievements: these may cover working experience, education, training, community service and other activities.

In your résumé, you are attempting to present yourself as an interesting and capable person, so you must impress the reader with your background by giving facts, not making general claims of competency.

Begin Each Achievement with an Action Verb

Searching your past for these facts and choosing the most suitable ones for your résumé is not easy. Also, it is often difficult to write about them clearly and briefly. One way to make it easier is to use action verbs, such as those in the following list:

achieved	directed	originated
attained	eliminated	participated in
audited	established	planned
averted	evaluated	prepared
awarded	guided	presented
built	improved	produced
coached	increased	rectified
compiled	initiated	revised
completed	instigated	saved
conceived	introduced	selected
corrected	learned	solved
created	managed	supervised
decreased	negotiated	tested
designed	obtained	trained
developed	organised	wrote

These should be placed at the beginning of sentences which describe something you have done. By using verbs in this way, you can avoid the repetitive 'I'. Few things give a worse impression on a page—be it your letter or résumé—than sentence after sentence starting with 'I'. Also, it can make you sound very self-centred.

You are now writing achievement statements which show how you produced outputs from your job tasks. The result is likely to show your ability to produce results, plus the wide range of your transferable skills. Review your list of achievement statements. Put them in order of importance by deciding their value to the job for which you are applying.

Your prioritised list of achievement statements is now ready to be screened for relevance to your job target. But first, before transferring your selection to your draft, consider which achievements are relevant to the three characteristics of almost any job role:

Communicating   **Efficiency**   **Data Management**

Make sure you transfer to your draft résumé achievement statements which demonstrate your abilities in these three.

Consider All Your Skills

Employers can quickly see whether you have suitable educational and technical skills for certain jobs by looking at the subjects you have studied, your results and where that study took place. Most job applicants, however, stop at that point and just add the names of past employers and job titles and so miss an opportunity to describe other valuable skills that their career record has given them.

The samples in this Guide are excellent models for you to learn from, since they incorporate many years of practical, professional experience and research in résumé preparation. Plus they all describe successful job seekers whose personal data has been changed to protect their privacy.

Consider what each one tells you about the applicant. Each shows an employer that the people who wrote them knew about hard work and responsibility and that they achieved something as a result.

If you read only the sample résumé(s) directly relating to your career goal, you will not obtain the full value from using this Guide. The facts stated in all the résumés are important because they tell an employer that the applicants have skills which can be transferred to their employment objective.

Obviously, not all jobs require the same skills. However, many skills are useful in all jobs. Examples include:

The ability:

- to communicate well (both verbally and in writing);
- to work towards objectives;
- to solve problems;
- to work within time limits and schedules.

Statements showing that you have acquired some or all of these skills will take time to prepare, but it is worth spending that time. The sample résumés in this Guide will help you.

Your Résumé ...

should be a forward-looking capabilities brief, not a backwards-looking story of your life.

Employment Record

The following paragraphs will help you compile the Employment Record section of your résumé.

Job title

This term is used for the name given to your position. In many cases you may not have had an official title, so it is up to you to define the job as clearly as possible with a suitable term.

There is no law which requires you to record in your résumé the job title allocated to you by current or past employers. You therefore have an opportunity to compose a term which conveys in the clearest possible way the nature of the job tasks you carried out. Using titles like Clerk, Administration Class 1 or Trainee Manager convey very little to the reader. Leave out terms such as Trainee, Junior, Intermediate or Senior. Designate yourself by what you did, such as Engineer, Book Designer, Personnel Officer, etc.

Think about the nature of the tasks you were engaged in and use a term which unambiguously conveys what you did.

I recently undertook an exercise to list all the job titles in use within the Human Resource Management family of job activities. By the time I had reached 38 I gave up. However, the exercise provided a wider range of titles to select from than I thought possible when I started the exercise. Consider researching the same for your occupation.

Nature of employer's business

A brief description—such as 'take-away food', 'timber merchants' or 'electrical goods wholesalers'—is all that is required here.

My major accomplishments, contributions or achievements

Outline the things you feel you did well in the job. Did you, for instance, increase sales or efficiency in some big or small way? Did you improve some part of the job? If so, inform your prospective employer in your résumé.

Résumé Writing Steps

1. Decide what job function or job role (not job title, as these vary from employer to employer) your résumé will target.

2. Undertake thorough self-assessment analysis with help of a career adviser or a career planning book.

3. Study samples of good résumés which have been successful in Australia.

4. Compile your fact sheet of dates (employment, graduation, awards) and computer software competencies before you draft your résumé.

5. Write 'free-form' for 10 minutes on why you want this job.

6. Select section headings and prepare your first draft with care.

7. Have a person you respect read it to provide feedback on style, content and design layout.

8. Audit résumé content against Steps 2, 3, 4 and 5 for extras worth including or changing.

9. Check spelling!

10. Revise, produce and mail unfolded (add Cover Letter).

11. Do not wait for results from one job application. Mail others to alternative targets.

What to Leave Out

You will need to decide to what degree you wish to share personal data with someone you have not yet met. My recommendation is that you leave out the following:

- Reasons for Leaving Previous Employers
- Your Citizenship
- Place of Birth
- Spouse's / Partner's Occupation
- Current or Past Remuneration Details
- Salary Expectations
- Religion
- Weight

- Height
- Health
- Photographs
- Untruths
- Weaknesses
- Children's Names and Ages
- Hobbies
- Marital Status
- Number of Children
- Details of Primary Education and Location of School

References and Referees

There are three ways of providing your references when you apply for a job:

1. You can attach copies of written references to your job application letter and résumé when you mail these to prospective employers;
2. You can make a statement in your résumé or letter that the names of referees will be provided on request or at your interview;
3. You can include near the end of your résumé—under a section headed 'Referees' or 'People Who Know Me Well'—a list of people who may be contacted by your prospective employers.

The first way is not recommended. The employer, realising that you will only include a written reference if it is good, may not be convinced that the references you have provided give the full picture of you as a person. References included with your letter take time to read and make your job application bulky. Often they are typed in different styles and tend to make your application look messy. Besides this, they may make you sound like a perfect person—which no one is! A better procedure is to take these references with you to an interview in case you are asked for them.

The second way is the easiest. It tells the employer that there are people who will give you a reference. It takes up very little space and avoids sending extra sheets of paper. This method allows the employer to tell you what type of referees he or she would like to contact. For example, some employers might prefer references from lecturers or teachers who know your learning abilities and habits; some might wish to contact people who supervised you at work; and others want references from people who know you through sporting or community activities.

The third way—that of including the names of referees in your résumé—is acceptable if you follow these steps:

- Name only two referees, or three at the most;
- Do not name a referee unless you have first made sure that the person is willing to talk about you to an employer if required;
- Include the referee's full name, occupation, address and telephone number—home and work;
- Choose referees who have had close contact with you or supervised you while you carried out your work. This is more important than whether the referee holds a high position.

Prospective employers will not always contact your referees, however your list is useful as it shows that you know people who can comment on your character and ability to work.

Letters of Commendation

A way to gain attention to your references is to take to an interview a letter of commendation or praise that you may have received. If you have articles published in newspapers or newsletters that show you in a good light, you may also strengthen your chances of being considered for a job. This sort of information is often bulky, which is why it should not accompany your job application in the mail but be kept in a folder to take to interviews.

Another way of avoiding the problem of sending photocopies of extra letters or clippings with your job application is to include short quotations from them in your résumé. You may have received letters praising your performance during work or school. If they have been written by managers, supervisors or teachers and if you feel that a short quotation would have a useful place in your résumé then include a sentence or two in a suitable section.

Spare Copies of Your Résumé

Take five or more spare copies with you when attending interviews. You are likely to meet more people than just the one with whom the interview appointment has been made.

At the beginning of each separate interview, hand the interviewer a copy of your résumé. It is likely that your original résumé has not been copied for the information of these additional interviewers.

If you are to meet an employer following an interview with a recruitment agency, it is also highly likely that your résumé has been re-written by the agency staff. My preference is for the employer interviewer to read my version of myself, not just some other person's interpretation of me. So make sure you hand across your version of yourself.

Other Uses for Your Résumé

You can use your résumé to help you prepare for the questions you are likely to be asked at an interview. Before each interview, read several times through the information you have given the employer in your résumé. You should know thoroughly by now what you have written and this will help you to answer the interviewer's questions with confidence.

A copy of your résumé should be sent to each of your referees so that they are familiar with exactly what types of employment you are seeking. A telephone call to brief them on specific vacancies you are pursuing is also useful and diplomatic. How can they best support your application unless they know what you are applying for?

When your job search is over, you can use your résumé for other purposes. Remember, you have written it as a statement of your achievements and your capability to earn money. Here are some further possible uses for your résumé:

- As additional information for a loan application to a bank, building society or finance company.
- As a useful summary of your achievements when applying for membership of professional associations, sporting or social clubs or community service organisations.
- As a support to accompany tertiary education applications (especially mature-age applicants), scholarships or sponsorships.
- As a character reference if you are ever summoned to court for an offence (ask your solicitor first).
- As a guide for friends who are starting to search for jobs and want help in designing their own résumés.

Store Your Résumé

File a copy of your completed résumé in a safe place. It is likely that you will change employers again or find it useful for internal job applications where you work. You can save time by referring to what worked best for you in the past.

REMINDER! One more time

Take a pen or a highlighter and, as you read through each and every résumé in this Guide. Mark where you observe:

- a layout that appeals to you;
- innovative use of section headings;
- information which matches (or is similar to) yours;
- words which you could adapt.

Only then, start the first draft of your résumé.

Golden Rules for Résumé Writing

- Write your information in terms of benefits to the employer, not the benefits you want.

- Describe your abilities, potential and things you can do for the employer by using your past experience as proof to support the claims you make.

- Emphasise how well you did your job tasks rather than leave this to conjecture.

- Tell what you accomplished rather than describe your responsibilities. They are not the same. Do this in terms of increased profits, money saved, production increased, procedures improved, etc.

- Explain long breaks in employment continuity in your covering letter.

- Avoid going into excessive detail about education and personal details.

- Avoid the use of such terms as 'synopsis of résumé', 'amplified résumé', 'confidential résumé'.

- Capitalise, centre or use bold print for section headings to emphasise information.

- Do not cram your résumé. It gives it a cluttered look and discourages readers.

- Leave plenty of white space on each page.

- Keep at least a 2.5 cm margin on either side of your paper.

- Paragraphs must be short. Double space between paragraphs.

- Do not date your résumé. You don't want this month's date on next month's mailings.

- How many children, dependants, relations you have adds no value to your résumé.

- Your health or sporting activities are good conversation items but take up precious space on your résumé—leave them out.

- Don't write too much about just one aspect of your eligibility.

- Workshops, seminars, part-time courses—current and in the past two years— are worthy of mention providing each relates usefully to doing the targeted job.

- Stress the new learning you have acquired and are pursuing.

- Emphasise your abilities and record of working well within teams of colleagues.

- Almost all jobs in existence require communication skills. Check that your résumé includes evidence of yours.
- Select those achievements which demonstrate you have the transferable skills required by the job and work unit you are targeting.

Remember, your résumé is a
60 second commercial
to convince others of your abilities
to solve their problems

2 Checklist for Your Résumé

Checking Over Your Résumé

When your résumé is in draft form, examine it closely as you read through the following checklists. You may be surprised to discover how worthwhile such a check can be. Even though you have already spent a lot of time and effort writing your résumé, you may find you need to make some important changes. If made now, such changes may save you losing opportunities for interviews.

Check your résumé carefully against each question. Answer the question by putting a tick in the relevant column. When you've finished the checklist, you'll know what parts need changing.

Structure

	✓	
	Yes	No
• Is your name at the top of each page?	❏	❏
• Does your career objective appear immediately below your name?	❏	❏
• Are your best points relevant to the career goal clearly described early in your résumé?	❏	❏
• Are your current address and telephone number included?	❏	❏
• Have you included an alternative phone number where a message may be left for you?	❏	❏
• Have you recorded specific achievements and experiences (and avoided writing a long autobiography)?	❏	❏
• Is your highest educational level shown first in the education section?	❏	❏

Career Objective

	✓	
	Yes	No
• Does your career objective clearly state what sort of work you want?	❑	❑
• Is this objective a true indication of your personal ambitions—neither too low nor too high in its aim?	❑	❑
• Have you succeeded in telling the employer what you'll give as well as what you want?	❑	❑
• Is it short, like those in the samples in this Guide?	❑	❑

Composition

	✓	
	Yes	No
• Do your words (wherever possible) show results you have achieved, problems you have dealt with and important learning experiences you have had?	❑	❑
• Have you mentioned any of your activities in the community that demonstrate your planning, teamwork, organising and communicating ability?	❑	❑
• Have you avoided including information on your religion, ethnic origin or citizenship?	❑	❑
• Have you avoided stating how much you expect to be paid?	❑	❑
• If you have decided to include your age, have you listed your date of birth rather than your present age?	❑	❑
• Have you used short statements and short paragraphs?	❑	❑
• Is your use of punctuation correct?	❑	❑
• Is the spelling correct?	❑	❑
• Have you avoided long words, business jargon and terms that you do not normally use?	❑	❑
• Do most of the statements in your résumé start with action verbs?	❑	❑
• Have you succeeded in using 'I' fewer than three times, if at all?	❑	❑
• Have you avoided being too shy or modest in describing yourself and your achievements?	❑	❑
• Have you removed all irrelevancies, such as your passport number, ages of your children?	❑	❑

3   Producing Your Résumé

Your résumé should be presented clearly. Having it typed is essential. It is best to use A4 paper (a standard business size). Use good quality, white, bond paper—unlined. The résumé should be typed on one side of the paper only. As well as at the top of the first page, your name should appear on each following page.

Find a computer operator with a high grade laser printer who is experienced and aware of ways to create an attractive page layout. Before you have your résumé typed, mention all the points in your résumé that you feel need to stand out or have special treatment. A skilled person will know how to use the technology to produce your résumé in an attractive, easy-to-read form. Asterisks, bold print, capitals, bullets, dashes and italics can all be used to highlight points.

Selecting the Presentation Style

a)   Attracting the Reader

When choosing a presentation style for your résumé, your main consideration should be readability. Unless your résumé is attractive to read, your application is unlikely to be considered. The following tips will assist you:

- Leave plenty of white space on each page—allow a margin of at least 2.5 cm all around and consider using indenting to keep the line length short (see examples below). About 8 to 10 words per line is a comfortable length in your résumé.
- Capitalise, centre and/or use bold print for section headings to make them stand out.
- Don't mix typefaces—just change the point size.
- Use standard white 80 gsm A4 paper (297 mm by 210 mm).
- Laser-printed copies are preferable to photocopies of originals
- Avoid italics—they are difficult to read.
- Avoid too much bold type—use bold for section headings and to emphasise specific words or phrases but not for whole paragraphs.
- Avoid using all capitals for whole paragraphs or lists of skills, etc. They are hard to read.

- Underlining should not be used—it interferes with the reader's ability to recognise the shape of words.
- Be consistent. Always allow the same amount of space between bullet points and before every section heading. Don't compromise just to fit more on the page. If it won't fit, revise your wording.

b) Selection of Typeface

There are two groups of typefaces: serif and sans serif. Serif typefaces have small ticks on each letter which enable the reader to distinguish them more easily. This book is in Palatino 11 pt—a serif typeface. Serif typefaces are best used when you have large amounts of text. The following examples show the same sentence in four different serif typefaces and, finally, one sans serif—Helvetica:

Palatino 12 pt:
- Directed the development of national advertising and promotional campaigns and materials, the majority produced in-house

Times 12 pt:
- Directed the development of national advertising and promotional campaigns and materials, the majority produced in-house

Times New Roman 12 pt:
- Directed the development of national advertising and promotional campaigns and materials, the majority produced in-house

New Century Schoolbook 12 pt:
- Directed the development of national advertising and promotional campaigns and materials, the majority produced in-house

Helvetica 12 pt:
- Directed the development of national advertising and promotional campaigns and materials, the majority produced in-house

Helvetica is not as easy to ready as the serif fonts but is an acceptable typeface for résumés which will be scanned (see page 24). All the above typefaces are the same point size but, as you can see, take up different amounts of space. If you have lots of information to put into your résumé, choose one of the smaller typefaces, i.e. Times or Times New Roman.

A Further Check

After your résumé has been produced, discuss its appearance with your transcriber. Can either of you see ways of improving it? Often you will find that a joint effort can produce a much more appealing design on the second attempt. Take the opportunity at this stage to examine the appearance of your résumé by working through the following checklist.

Appearance

✓

Yes No

- Is your résumé neatly and accurately typed? Is it free from errors and marks caused by corrections? ❑ ❑
- Is the résumé clearly set out and concise? ❑ ❑
- Do your section headings stand out through the use of capital letters and/or bold print? ❑ ❑
- Is it typed on only one side of each page? ❑ ❑
- Is the résumé on A4 paper (297 mm by 210 mm)? ❑ ❑
- Is it designed with wide margins and space between paragraphs? ❑ ❑
- Has its appearance been checked against the styles of the samples in this Guide? ❑ ❑

Pause! Just one more task before it is mailed—an easy one. Leave your résumé alone for 24 hours. Review it one more time the next day, make any changes you consider necessary and then reproduce it!

Final Check After Typing

✓

Yes No

- Are you satisfied that your résumé says everything concisely about you relevant to your employment goal? ❑ ❑
- Have you found a good quality photocopying machine that will make copies on A4 paper or do you have access to a high quality laser printer? ❑ ❑
- Have you purchased envelopes suitable for A4 paper so that your résumé can be posted without being folded? ❑ ❑
- Have you used the Résumé Critique Form on page 23? ❑ ❑
- Do others feel that your résumé is an interesting summary of your preparation for employment and one that shows you deserve to be considered? ❑ ❑

Résumé Trimming Techniques

Delete

- Résumé of ...
- Your middle name or initial
- Job titles for positions you held more than five years ago
- Any reasons given for leaving jobs
- Page number

Alter

- Substitute an action verb for the words 'responsible for'
- Cancel out one Section Heading and transfer the data to another suitable one
- Change full dates, e.g. 8/10/96 to 20/12/97 to duration of time, i.e. 14 months
- Reduce the margins on the left and right of each page (2 cm minimum)
- Reduce the size of the font (10 point minimum)

Photocopying or Laser-printed Copies

Only when you are satisfied with your résumé's final form will you be prepared to spend money on the next stage—having it photocopied.

When you begin applying for jobs, it is quite suitable to send a photocopy of your résumé. (Your application letter, on the other hand, should always be an original: never send a copy.) When copying your résumé, make sure you use a high quality photocopier to get the best possible result. After all, you've spent a great deal of effort making sure your résumé looks good—don't spoil it by sending a second-rate photocopy. The way you present yourself to prospective employers is very important. The standard of appearance of your letter and résumé can say a lot about you.

Résumé Critique Form

Ask no fewer than three people to read your résumé and record their scores before you use it for job applications.

Rate the résumé on the points shown below, scoring from a low of 1 to a high of 3 in each of the items listed.

Item	Score 1	2	3
1. **Overall Appearance** Is it easy to read quickly?			
2. **Layout** Does it look professional and well typed? Do key points stand out?			
3. **Length** Could the résumé tell the same story if it were shortened?			
4. **Relevance** Has irrelevant information been eliminated?			
5. **Writing Style** Is it easy to get a picture of me from the contents?			
6. **Action Orientation** Do most sentences and paragraphs begin with action verbs?			
7. **Precision** Does it avoid generalities and focus on specific information about my experience, projects, results?			
8. **Accomplishments** Are my accomplishments and skills emphasised?			
9. **Completeness** Is all the important information included?			
10. **Bottom Line** How well does my résumé accomplish its purpose of getting the employer to invite me for an interview?			
Rating Point Total			
Grand Total (30 maximum)			

What are some other ways that you would suggest I improve this résumé?

When Agencies or Employers Use a Scanner

Many résumés today no longer have to pass a 20-second skim read by a person in a recruitment role who is sorting them into two piles: reject and possible. Instead, more and more firms—both Employment Agencies and in-company Human Resources Departments—are scanning résumés and using computer software to produce shortlists of staff 'eligible' for emerging vacancies.

When a résumé is received by the Human Resources Department, it is put into a scanner. The scanner takes an 'electronic photo', referred to as the résumé 'image' and sends this image to text by using Optical Character Recognition (OCR) software. Once in text form, applicant data, such as name, education and degrees, job titles and skill words—keywords which describe the kinds of experience you have had—can be extracted and put in fields called the 'Applicant Summary'. The Human Resource Management person can then search on any combination of fields and keywords to find a match for a current job role vacancy.

To make sure that electronic reading of their résumés is an asset rather than a liability, applicants generally put a 'Keyword Summary' close to their career objective. Think about how the employer has described the vacancy. Your résumé should contain the same keywords that appear in the description of the vacancy, otherwise your application may be overlooked.

Electronic Résumés Require New Writing Techniques

Here are a few tips on how to prepare a résumé for the electronic recruiter:

1. Print your résumé on a laser printer. Don't waste money on special bond paper, matching envelopes or any colour deviance from plain white. Your résumé will be scanned, then photocopied or faxed or emailed to the manager with the vacancy, defeating any special paper efforts.
2. Use standard typefaces such as Helvetica, Palatino or Times New Roman.
3. Use a font size 10 to 16 point.
4. Learn to think and write your résumé in terms of nouns, not verbs. Action words like designed, implemented and launched are out. In scannable résumés, nouns dominate. Computers search for keywords such as sales, purchasing and manager. For example, if you are a teacher in a school system but would like to be a corporate trainer, then use a word like 'training' to describe your recent work.
5. An extension of the noun concept, keywords are also called buzzwords or descriptors. Keywords are what employers search for when trying to fill a position. The more keyword marketing

points you present about yourself in your résumé, the more likely you are to be selected from an electronic database.

6. Do not use a two-column format. Use a résumé format with your name at the top, your contact information on a line or so below, followed by job objective, qualifications, work experience and training experience, etc.

7. Avoid fancy graphics, such as vertical and horizontal lines and boxes as they do not scan well and may cause your résumé to be misinterpreted.

8. You may want to submit your résumé three ways: via facsimile which you assume will be computer-scanned, by email as a text file and finally as a conventional letter of application and résumé.

Portfolios

Writers, artists and photographers have assembled portfolios rather than résumés for many years. Now the portfolio approach to employers is fast becoming the appropriate assertive way for many other categories of job seekers to present themselves as the best candidate for employment. Your résumé can be used to introduce you and your portfolio as a method of communicating more about you in an interest-arousing manner. You can record on your résumé that your portfolio is available on request or mention its availability in your covering letter. Alternatively, it can be taken to an interview and left with the interviewer to review at its conclusion. A further strategy is to attend the first interview and follow up with your portfolio, having adjusted its contents after you have learned more about the job role and employment environment.

Using a portfolio approach can chronicle details and examples of your expertise, endorsements from others about your abilities and illustrate your transferable skills. It provides you with an opportunity to expand on your claims in your résumé. It can be developed and presented in print format, as an electronic work or as mixed-media.

Our career patterns are usually a collection of various forms of work rather than a linear history of trainee to senior responsibilities in the same occupation, same industry. The trend is for employers to appreciate this pattern more. Portfolios give us the liberty of showing the linkages between what may be diverse forms of work we have experienced, the transferability of skills from one career direction content to another. It is evidence of flexibility that more employers are now seeking in their recruits. With more job roles demanding multi-tasking features, flexible work assignments and short-term projects, the portfolio careerist can advance their case by evidence of their past experiences assembled with thought and care. The flexibility of the portfolio approach allows you to group and re-order the evidence of your talents to match the changing direction of your personal career journey.

You can assemble and index charts, graphs, letters of commendation, copies of performance appraisals, extracts from speeches or reports you have written, certificates, awards, work samples, creative samples, evidence of your project planning and management skills. You could include a mind mapping illustration or a plan you used to solve a problem at work, in fact, anything which is relevant to enhancing why the employer should employ you. The key is the word 'relevant'. Relevant to the needs of the particular employer to whom you are applying. For example, your Year 10 Best Sportsperson Award copy has no place in your portfolio unless you are applying to the Australian Institute of Sport or other sports-related organisation.

Your challenge is what to include and how to arrange the contents. Sample of letters, memos, news clips, photos and so on may have a place in your assembly. Several guides have been published about assembling portfolios. The career researcher and author, Martin Kimeldorf, produces the best in my opinion. I know him well and admire his care in his recommendations. Martin's *Portfolio Power* is published by Peterson's.

No employer is interested in
what you want
until interest is created in
what you can offer

4   Sample Résumés

Easy-to-Find Index

Résumés for Special Situations

Résumés for Career Changes

Résumés for Specific Occupations

Résumés for Specific Occupations continued

Isobel Browne

151 Russell Street
Balmain 2041

Tel: (02) 9818 1564 (Home)
(02) 9267 1122 (Office)

OBJECTIVE

To be employed in Human Resource Management utilising and building upon my skills and expertise

CAREER ACHIEVEMENTS

- Successfully managed a Career Transition Program for 85 surplus staff

- Successfully managed a team of Human Resource Specialists in an organisation of 755 employees

- Project managed the introduction of an Employee Assistance Program

- Project managed the introduction of autonomous work teams

- Developed and conducted training courses in Change Management

PRECIS OF MAJOR ATTRIBUTES

- **Working with people** — my experience in advising, guiding, assisting people to realise their potential through self-analysis and identification of appropriate development interventions

- **People management** — enjoy working with and leading people and the challenge of developing teams

- **Organisation and planning** — depth of experience in project management has developed these skills

- **Knowledge of the HR environment** — am a generalist with specialist knowledge in recruitment and selection, training and change management

- **Communication** — experience in implementing strategic communications using a variety of media (print/poster/intranet)

- **Computer literacy and office management skills** — skilled in Microsoft Word for Windows, Excel and Microsoft Project and PowerPoint

Isobel Browne   **Page 2**

CAREER SUMMARY

12 months as Project Leader, Restructuring Transition Group

16 years in Personnel Management related fields

- Strategic Human Resource Manager in a developed organisational structure of 1,100 trade, professional and clerical staff engaged in building maintenance

- Managed specialist HR functions:
  - Industrial Relations at workplace level
  - Recruitment policy and procedures
  - OHS and Rehabilitation management

- Generalist Personnel Manager with recruitment, organisational development and change management skills

- Personnel Officer with 1,720 on payroll

- Recruitment Officer for technical and professional scientific positions

COURSES ATTENDED

- Currently in Year 2 part-time of Professional Diploma of Human Resources through Australian Human Resources Institute

- Performance Management Improvement Program conducted through University of Sydney over 12 weeks

- Managing for Change, an Open Learning Program for Middle Managers, conducted through University of New South Wales, successfully completed

PROFESSIONAL ASSOCIATIONS

- Associate Fellow, Australian Institute of Management

- Member, Australian Human Resources Institute

ELAINE CABLE

Unit 15, 459 St Kilda Road   Tel: 9648 3975
ST KILDA VIC 3182   Email: e.richards@msn.com.au

EMPLOYMENT OBJECTIVE

To apply my knowledge and skills in Payroll and Personnel Administration
matters in either part-time or full-time capacity, preferably located in the St Kilda
region. This could be a temporary or permanent position.

MAIN CAPABILITY AREAS

- Employee Records Maintenance
- Plant Production Efficiency Reports
- Petty Cash Management
- Workers Compensation Claims
- Absenteeism, Labour Turnover Analysis
- Payroll Administration

PERSONAL PROFILE

A self-motivated, dedicated person with a positive attitude and able to observe
confidentiality

Am a good team member on projects yet capable of working independently on
difficult tasks

A proven track record of achieving results through managing and advising
people

Planning, organising and communicating together with an eye for detail are key
skills offered to an employer

Thrive on new opportunities

Have a good sense of humour

EMPLOYMENT SUMMARY

PETER SMITH CLOTHING PTY LTD   **18 YEARS 8 MONTHS**
(Clothing Manufacturers)

Payroll Management and Office Administration
- Responsible for weekly payroll for 105 employees—Lend Lease CAS PAY system
- Maintained personnel records and statistics
- Processed all workers' compensation claims
- Completed weekly analysis of production figures and produced plant efficiency report
- Completed month-to-date and year-to-date plant efficiency spreadsheets detailing:
  - Headcount
  - Production units
  - Downtime
  - Manufacturing days
  - Capacity usage bonus %
  - Net efficiency
- Prepared monthly report for the Human Resources Director detailing labour turnover, hours worked, absenteeism, workers' compensation claims and other matters of note
- Acted as secretary for the Consultative Committee. Prepared and distributed Minutes to Management Clothing Trade Union Consultative Committee and all employees
- Arranged Company functions and liaised with Management about them
- Counselled employees in matters which reflected on their work performance on an informal basis
- Promoted and controlled purchasing of company products in-house increasing sales
- Experienced with accounts payable and debtors

CAREER DEVELOPMENT LEARNING EXPERIENCES

- Completed a number of training courses including such subjects as Database and Spreadsheets Lotus 1.2.3 and EXCEL
- Experience on Microsoft Word Processing and WordPerfect 6.0

Consultative Committee

Secretarial support over five years with agenda covering employee grievances, enterprise agreement content, staff communications

REFEREES WILL BE PROVIDED ON REQUEST

JON DAVIS

CAREER OBJECTIVE

To utilise my senior management, research, planning, organisation, coordination, budgeting, team leadership, creative and communication skills and my international direct marketing and publishing industry experience at a senior level

CAREER ACHIEVEMENTS

1973 - 1998   **Peterson's Business & Trade Publishing**
- As *South Pacific Director*, arrested slide in market declining at over 18,000 customers per annum, including:
  - defining market expectations and establishing benchmarks
  - analysing existing market strengths and weaknesses
  - identifying areas of opportunity
  - establishing evaluation groups for suggested alternatives
  - drafting and implementing 12 month action plan for each country
  - defining responsibilities and authorities
  - establishing accepted timetable
  - coordinating four printing plants resources
  - setting up individual promotions

  increasing new customers from 32,000 to over 45,000 and increasing existing customers from 155,000 to 160,000

- As *Marketing Director, Australia*
  - evaluated international trends in direct marketing industry
  - identified immediate opportunities for new products and new channels
  - introduced new products and additional mailing opportunities
  - identified additional opportunities to utilise existing database
  - adopted more aggressive promotional activities
  - restructured team including consolidation of operations department and introduction of new talent through key appointments
  - streamlined promotion process

  increasing profit from $22m to over $40m per annum, reducing staff numbers from 75 to 63, saving over $1m per annum, reducing promotional lead time from 24 weeks to 14 weeks

- As *Associate Director, Tradesmen's Books and Special Books*, produced nearly 35% of company's $2,500m revenue:
  - setting up stronger, better balanced publishing program
  - improving customer retention through communication of global breakthroughs
  - improving promotion strength through global cooperative testing
  - extending product range into Nordic Countries and Europe
  - increasing number of new book customers

- coordinating international appeal of products without losing local country appeal *increasing global book revenue by nearly 50% from $473m to $697m, raising international book profit from $90m to $132m*

- As *Product Manager, Books Special Series Books* marketed in South Pacific to $47m per annum:
  - translating strategies into detailed action plans
  - initiating expansion of book catalogue business
  - broadening profit base
  - launching two new book series
  - strengthening publishing program with best of local and international books
  made books number one profit earner, lifting operating profit by nearly 40%

pre 1973   **Editing and Pre-Press Trainee** positions in United Kingdom

EDUCATIONAL QUALIFICATIONS

1970   **Bachelor of Arts (Hons) Economics**
                                University of Wessex, United Kingdom

1991   **Leadership Program**
                                Center for Business Management, Colorado, USA

1992   **Fundamentals of Finance and Accounting for Non Finance Executives**
                                Wharton School, USA

1992   **Time Management**
                                Priority Management, USA

1996   **Leadership for Growth**
                                Center for Executive Development, USA

CONTACT DETAILS

Address: 58 Paddington Street
                                PADDINGTON NSW 2021

Telephone: (02) 9360 4462 (Private)

Email: jon.d@ifp.net.au

Melinda Fredrikson

21/315-319 New South Head Road, Double Bay 2028
Tel: 9358 4111 (w) or 9328 1482 (h)

CAREER OBJECTIVE

To utilise my organisational skills in the Media Department of an Advertising Agency and continue my studies in advertising, building a career in Media Planning and Buying

SUMMARY OF SKILLS

Planning/Organising
Created monthly product sales graphs and tables using Microsoft Excel
Conducted survey of client database
Planned direct marketing for workshops
Created numerous spreadsheets using Excel
Responsible for purchase of all office stationery and supplies, including researching for best price deals
Maintained accounts and invoicing daily
Used initiative to solve problems when left alone in charge of office
Demonstrated ability to work to deadlines

People/Sales
Exceeded monthly sales target 5 times in 8 month period
Increased average monthly product sales
Established excellent customer relations base
Promoted new products via targeted mailings

Creative
Designed 10 page workshop handout
Created advertising material for direct marketing
Produced distributors' newsletter
Created overhead transparencies

Software Applications
Competent on both Macintosh and Windows, using the following programs:
- Microsoft Word 6
- Microsoft Excel 5 (spreadsheet)
- FileMaker Pro 3.1 (invoicing, database)
- ReadySetGo 6.0
- PowerPoint
- QuarkXPress 3.32
- Quicken (Accounts)

Melinda Fredrikson   2

RELEVANT TRAINING AND EDUCATION

- East Sydney Institute of TAFE: July 1997—Current
  Advertising Certificate III

- DFM Training Institute: Marketing Course   May—June 1997

- Computer Solutions: Microsoft Excel 5.0   February 1997

- Sydney Evening College: Typing Course   October 1996

- Seaforth TAFE: Visual Perception & Expression Class   Feb—July 1994

- Narrabeen High School: Year 11   Completed in 1993

- Forest High School: School Certificate   Completed in 1992

EMPLOYMENT SUMMARY

Working Life Options Pty Ltd   **June 1996—Current**
Career Development Consultants
Position: Assistant
Part-time from June 1994—Sept 1995 and Full-time since June 1996

Docall Pty Ltd   **January—June 1996**
Authorised Mobile Phone Retailers
Position: Sales Consultant

Elizabeth Redman Fashions Ltd   **February—December 1995**
Fashion Retail
Position: Retail Assistant (part-time casual)

Other casual work experiences have included market research interviewing
and waitressing

PERSONAL INFORMATION

Enjoy music and literature... swimming...go to the gym regularly...would like
to travel overseas...love meeting new people

References available on request

Ian Smithson

23 Inaminka Road
Milton 4064
Fax: (07) 3359 4881

Telephone: (07) 3360 4111 (B)
(07) 3361 4413 (H)
0419 708 914 (Mobile)

Objective—Client Services

To apply skills gained as a professional Education and Training Project Manager to a Client Services and/or Project Management position for a company whose core business is training and which specialises in the Hospitality sector of the economy.

Career Summary

Employed in both public and private sectors. Proven track record in the field of Education and Training. Skilled in training delivery, training material development and training project management. More recently specialised in large scale computer systems implementation projects—latest being SAP.

Professional Development

Associate Diploma in Adult Education (will complete a Bachelor of Adult Education in November 1998)

Professional Development

- Presentation Skills (8 days)
- Train the Trainer
- Negotiation Skills
- Advanced Training Skills
- Consultancy Skills
- Essentials of Management
- Staff Counselling
- MS Project
- MS Word, PowerPoint and Excel
- Various SAP Courses

Professional Career Record

BORDER PETROLEUM AUSTRALIA — MARCH 1992 TO PRESENT

Responsibilities

- Training strategy design and planning
- Project management
- Training material development
- Trainer training (coach training)
- Ongoing training strategy development and implementation

Major Achievements

- Successfully obtained approval from the executive to proceed with ongoing training strategy which included the establishment of dedicated training resources in each region
- In 1997 was part of a highly successful project team responsible for implementing SAP in Australia and New Zealand. Was involved in the design, development and implementation of training materials. Numbers trained will be approximately 1,500
- Initiated a national review of Trainer Accreditation policy. Trained trainers nationally. Set up administration of Accreditation Policy.

TOO GOOD COMPUTING — 1989 TO 1992

Responsibilities

- Training material development (mainframe training project)
- Procedural documentation development and implementation

Major Achievements

- Managed a small team in the development of procedural documentation used by users of a large Insurance System

AUSTRALIAN TAXATION OFFICE — 1978 TO 1988

Responsibilities

- Training Officer—delivering programs such as Counter Officer's course, Time Management, Supervision, Staff Counselling
- Counter Officer

Major Achievements

- Established a Computer Training facility and function at the Australian Taxation Office
- Developed and delivered many successful training programs

Barbara Jacobs

149 Hall Street, Dandenong 3195
Email barbaraj@gateway.com.au
Tel (03) 9365 3517

OBJECTIVE

To be appointed Change Agent and Learning Development Coordinator for a well reputed company in Information Technology sector

REPRESENTATIVE SAMPLE OF MY ACHIEVEMENTS

Customer Service Change

Led an organisational change initiative designed to change employees' attitudes with a view to improving customer service, quality and productivity by:

- Designing and conducting focus groups for employees and customers to obtain feedback on customer service issues and to discuss solutions
- Reporting to management, employees and customers on customer needs and concerns

Workplace Analysis and Socio-Technical Systems Analysis

Investigated human factors contributing to plant failures and other productivity issues Participated in a multi-disciplinary team comprising management and operating crews from a power station. The project resulted in:

- changes to the ergonomic layout of the Plant Control Room which had previously created confusion in emergencies
- identification of the link between the psychological and physiological stress arising out of shift patterns which had resulted in major plant errors
- review of inter-shift and intra-shift communication systems

Psychological Testing

Investigated the feasibility of introducing psychological testing in Southern Electric for the purposes of senior management development, succession planning, recruitment and career counselling. My work involved:

- researching the introduction of Assessment Centres for senior management development and for fast tracking high potential candidates
- modifying procedures for recruiting Engineering Cadets
- administering and scoring intelligence and personality test

Attidudinal/Climate Surveys

Managed attitudinal surveys about employee issues such as shift patterns, semi-autonomous teams and internal communication. Outcomes of conducting the surveys and implementing changes based on the results included:

- introduction of information and training sessions after identifying that employees knew little about a management initiative known as 'semi-autonomous teams'

Performance Development Tool

Designed development tool to enhance Southern Electric's performance appraisal system. Managers had been experiencing difficulty administering the existing process and conducting appraisal interviews. Features of the improvement included:

- employee's strengths and weaknesses are ranked by both employees and employer against the relevance of particular skills to the job
- employee's essential development needs are highlighted
- facilitates more open discussion between the employee and employer

Job Evaluation and Performance Pay

Designed a performance-based pay matrix to build upon the existing job evaluation system

Benchmarking

Represented Southern Electric in an external Benchmarking study on Communication coordinated by the Australian Quality Council. The study has highlighted some of the soft measures considered crucial to successful communication practices in large organisations

Career Pathing

Assisted in the design of a performance-based career path model for the Commercial Group at Belgrove Power Station. This involved:

- identifying the competencies required for each salary band within each job
- developing criteria for evaluating performance to allow progress to the next salary band

OTHER TRAINING

Executive Development Program	Monash University
Quality Management Systems	Australian Quality Council
Job Analysis & Evaluation Workshop	Drake Pty Ltd
Statistics and Their Application in the Workplace	RMIT

References provided on request

PHILIP MITCHELL

54 Barnet Close, West Hobart TAS 7004
Telephone: (03) 6241 3992 (H)

OBJECTIVE

To provide excellent counselling and consultancy services in a career services consultancy using my substantial background experience and training in counselling, career counselling and change management

SUMMARY OF COMPETENCE

INDIVIDUAL COUNSELLING—training in psychology and counselling and three years experience with Lifeline, as well as the management of a range of community-based clients for projects funded across Australia

CAREER COUNSELLING—am currently completing further graduate study in the field of adult career development at the University of Wollongong

HUMAN RESOURCE DEVELOPMENT—recent experience in this area in management and promotion of Employee Assistance Program

DESIGN OF SELF-HELP PROGRAMS—particularly as applied to the issues of healthy lifestyles and environmentally responsible behaviour

NETWORKING/NEGOTIATION—successful liaison with a wide range of client groups inside and outside government to achieve practical outcomes in areas linked to social change and organisational development

PROFESSIONAL ASSOCIATIONS

Australian Association of Career Counsellors
Australian National Network of Counsellors
Australian Association for Psychological Type

EDUCATION

Graduate Certificate in Adult Career Development, University of Wollongong, 1997 (current distance learning student—will complete mid-1998)

Major in Psychology, Australian National University, 1978—79 (three distinctions and one credit in second and third year psychology)

EMPLOYMENT HISTORY

1991—1998
Commonwealth Department of Housing and Regional Development
Administrative Service Officer Class 6, Human Resource Management

1986—1991
Commonwealth Department of the Arts, Education Unit

1982—1986
Commonwealth Department of Health, health education policy and programs

SKILLS AND ACHIEVEMENTS

Counselling and Group Work

- Counselled a range of clients (many in crisis situations) through three years part-time counselling experience with Lifeline (telephone and in-person) and participated in the counsellor education program run by Lifeline (as both a presenter and participant)

- Have organised and run a variety of workshops life management education targeted at educators in secondary schools.

Adult Career Development Practice

- Ability to use, and knowledge of, career development theories in career counselling, counselling theories and associated techniques and a wide range of career assessment instruments used in career counselling

- Ability to explore client's fears and emotions regarding the transition process, and ability to collaborate with clients in identifying personal goals and formulating action plans

- Ongoing professional development as a member of the Australian Association of Career Counsellors

Human Resource Development

- Managed and promoted the Employee Assistance Program in the Commonwealth Department of Housing and Regional Development

- Researched new approaches for performance appraisal for ASO 1-6 staff

KATE ENDERBY

25 Bathurst Court   Phone: (BH) 08 8332 3911
Alberton SA 5064   (H) 08 8321 4932

Career Summary

As a geologist, I have wide experience in minerals exploration and research, and have completed a PhD. The combination of industry and academic experience has been invaluable in giving me the background necessary to initiate and successfully undertake industry-orientated research. Postdoctoral work involved the new application of a technique of isotopic dating and the selling of this method to the minerals exploration industry.

Research and Analytical Skills

- Highly developed research and analytical skills which have involved the application of the 40Ar/39Ar dating technique to determine the age of minerals formed in gold and base metal deposits. This application of the dating method during postdoctoral research was the first in Australia and one of the first in the world
- Research and analytical skills were fully developed during PhD studies

Organisational and Planning Ability

- Used to working to tight time schedules in terms of completing quarterly and annual reports, and preparing and presenting half-yearly seminars for industry sponsors
- Completed a PhD in three years
- While a PhD student at the Australian National University, organised a years' geological research at the University of Reno, Nevada, USA
- While in exploration, supervised field assistants and drillers largely under difficult field conditions and, during academic work, supervised technical staff

Liaison Skills

- Have liaised between mining companies and academics and this liaison has resulted in a successful, ongoing research program
- Have been able to work with very difficult people and undertake industry-orientated research in an environment which is largely unsupportive of such endeavours

Communication Skills

High standard of oral and written communication developed through preparation and presentation of conference papers, seminars and reports for industry sponsors, short course presentations and notes for students and the writing of scientific proposals. Have published scientific papers in Australian and international journals. Communication skills have been enhanced by service on executive committees of non-government organisations (View Club and Amnesty International). Have a high standard of keyboard skills, and have had extensive use of Macintosh computer programs.

Qualifications

- PhD in Geology, Australian National University, 1990 (undertook 1 year of research at the University of Nevada, Reno, USA as part of this degree)
- BSc (1st class Hons, Geology), University of Sydney, 1981
- Participated in professional development workshops on women and leadership (1991), and Negotiation Skills for Women (1994)

Employment Record

Research Scientist, Geology Department and Research School of Earth Sciences, University of South Australia, Adelaide, 1989 to present

Exploration Geologist, RGI Ltd, Australia and Fiji, 1988

Exploration Geologist, AG Smith Minerals, Western Australia and NSW, 1982 to 1984

Geological Assistant, BHP Coal Division, Melbourne, VIC, 1980 to 1981 (vacation)

Professional Societies

Geological Society of Australia
Geological Society of America

Personal

Interests include politics, travel, film, aerobics, bushwalking, reading, art and issues involving status of women. Am a member of View Club, a non-government service organisation dedicated to improving the legal, political and professional status of women and Amnesty International.

EXECUTIVE APPOINTMENT PROSPECTUS

of

DAVID LEES

*'Specifications of what I seek, why I merit it
and what I have to offer.'*

OBJECTIVE

To apply my well-honed skills in the analysis and synthesis of volume data and the preparation of bases for negotiations and conflict resolution, and my extensive knowledge and practical experience in the legal field to the resolution of significant commercial and industrial issues.

This can be:
- by way of specific project assignment;
- as team member of a senior management task force;
- as an executive of a major industry or commercial entity.

STRENGTHS

I am able to offer a blend of attributes that combine dependability with commercial acumen. Exposure through legal work in many industries:

HEALTH	NURSING
MARITIME	AIRLINES
TRANSPORT	CLOTHING
WATERFRONT / STEVEDORING	LIQUOR
FURNISHING	FAST FOOD / RESTAURANT

QUALIFICATIONS

Master of Laws, University of Western Australia, 1988

BCom / BLLB, University of Sydney, 1987

CAREER

Chemist's delivery boy and shop assistant from aged 13 through to end of formal studies. Also mail sorter, farm hand, factory production line packer, barman and drinks waiter, and sewerage maintenance worker whilst funding tertiary studies.

Administrative Assistant to Industrial Relations Manager, Pongrass Industries Australia. Also Research Assistant to two Professors undertaking legal text publications.

Commenced practice as a Barrister at the NSW Bar 1989, practising in industrial, employment and administrative law.

KEY SKILLS

- Marshalling and organising large amounts of data.

- Communicating orally in an articulate, convincing and readily understandable manner.

- Distilling issues from complex material and expressing those issues in simple terms.

- Researching, investigating and analysing information with thoroughness and efficiency.

- Mixing and communicating effectively with a wide cross-section of people from the factory floor to the boardroom.

- Recognising the limits of my ability and knowing when to seek assistance.

- Understanding and digesting information concerning a diverse range of subject matters.

- Demonstrating resourcefulness when confronted with a difficult or unusual situation.

- Developing strategies, systems and procedures to facilitate the most efficient and expeditious completion of tasks.

PROFESSIONAL DEVELOPMENT EXPERIENCES

- Established a successful practice at the Bar in the field of Industrial and Administrative Law and achieved recognition as a competent industrial practitioner.

- Appeared in a large number of significant and complex industrial cases before the Industrial Tribunals of the country in the last five years.

- Attained the status of preferred Junior Counsel for the leader of the Industrial Bar in Australia.

- Formulated a plan for the presentation of extensive material in the Visiting Social Worker Officers case; that plan facilitated a ready understanding of the parties' positions and of developments with respect to each of the issues before the tribunal.

- As Junior Counsel assisting the Agent Orange Royal Commission I was responsible for the management of all data associated with the toxicity of the chemicals used in Vietnam.

- Motivated people to take or not to take courses of action or stances, especially with respect to difficulties confronted in personal relationships. I believe that I am a person that others feel that they can turn to in a time of need and get useful advice, assistance or support.

PROFESSIONAL DEVELOPMENT EXPERIENCES continued

- Formed and led a Residents' Action Group against the Woollahra Council and hospital developers to stop the over-development of a community hospital

- Managed the people in the Concept Residents Action Group with their different and sometimes conflicting interests and approaches to the resolution of the difficulty.

- Designed a system for the regulation of clothing industry outworkers in the form of a draft Award that was ultimately certified by the Industrial Relations Commission.

OTHER FACTS

Born 24 October 1963 ... Married with two children ... Resident of 57 Bathurst Street, Woollahra, Sydney Tel: (02) 9369 1524.

EXECUTIVE APPOINTMENT PROSPECTUS

of

DANIEL NORRIS

POSITION SOUGHT

Assistant to the Chief Executive Officer or Finance Director with primary responsibility for undertaking investigative and analysis tasks relating to commercial evaluations and new business ventures.

Alternatively:

a) Merchant Banking or Corporate Financial Services

b) Business Development

c) Treasury and Finance

STRENGTHS

I am able to offer an organisation a blend of skills that combines sound financial management with the commercial acumen needed to achieve growth.

Significant strengths include:

a) While being analytical and paying attention to detail, take a sound business overview.

b) Project orientated with a capacity for hard work and a high level of integrity.

c) Considered to be very thorough, conscientious and extremely persistent.

MAJOR SKILLS

a)   Creating a business from a concept.

b)   Ability to work up an acquisition prospect in its entirety.

c)   Investigating, analysing and reviewing new business proposals.

d)   Strategic analysis and rationalisation of a business.

e)   Systems review and design.

f)   Managing the finance and accounting functions.

g)   Turning around under-performing financial departments.

KEY ACHIEVEMENTS

AT CORTINGS INC.:

a)   Researched a business concept, prepared the Board proposal, then cold started the business in its entirety including personally recruiting all staff; designing the operations and financial systems; negotiating lines of finance; establishing an international network; instructing solicitors in the preparation of contracts; coordinating the preparation of marketing brochures and in due course selling to senior corporate executives.

b)   Carried out merger and acquisition studies of prospective candidates in Australia, UK and USA.

c)   Turned around the accounting department of a division and introduced accounting and financial disciplines and systems.

AT PATRICKS INTERNATIONAL:

a)   Developed corporate planning policies and procedures.

b)   Introduced the use of financial modelling with personal computers.

AT CLAYMORE'S PTY LTD:

a)   Financially managed a company through a severe recessionary period.

b)   Recommended restructuring three businesses involving the progressive rationalisation of product lines and the closure of one business.

c)   Established an internal audit department staffed with Chartered Accountants who were subsequently promoted to line positions.

EDUCATION AND TRAINING

Place	From	To	Examinations & Qualifications
University of Melbourne	1992	1993	Master of Commerce —Banking and Finance
Wharton School of Business		1987	Mergers and Acquisitions
		1984	Chartered Accountant (Aust.)

PERSONAL INFORMATION

Address: PO Box 519
                            Toorak VIC 3142
                            Australia

Email: dnorris@bigpond.com.au

Telephone: (61 3) 9909.2104

APPENDIX

JOB CONTENT

> *'The key requirement is that the quality and status of the tasks to be performed are of a high order.'*

These tasks should predominantly have a forward looking emphasis, that is establishing or developing, rather than historical review and control.

The demands of me will ensure the use of my investigative, information organising, conceptualising, systems review, analytical and commercial skills. Investigative analysis tasks would preferably take in and include holistic commercial evaluations.

As I am strongly task orientated and have a need for variety, the job should be challenging and project based. It should require attention to detail with an emphasis on quality and consequently will be one with lead times that allow for considered decision making.

There should be a requirement for travel, preferably internationally.

There will not be a requirement for the general management of people from diverse backgrounds unless when assigned to me in a project management situation. Similarly, while there will be an ability to present data and proposals to executives of organisations, it will not be a selling role.

EMPLOYMENT ENVIRONMENT

> *'The key requirement is the right partnership relationship with my boss and that this results in me being at the coal face and fully informed.'*

There is a need to work as part of a small team with similar skills and outlook, namely a small group of professionals or managers at corporate level.

The environment should reflect a level of comfort, status and standing.

To obtain maximum productivity I prefer to work with professional and technical associates, rather than emotional reactors. The environment will be decisive and not one characterised by management by committees and extensive meetings.

The organisation is likely to reward effort, have high standards and be slightly conservative. It will not be overly political but have an overriding respect for the individual that results in the development of its managers.

The organisation will be part of an industry that is developing or will itself be exposed to one that is. It is likely to be in the service sector and of medium size.

STYLE OF BOSS

'The key requirements of this relationship are that he/she:
* *involves me fully as an active participant and not as a subcontractor for partial assignments.*
* *encourages risk taking and looking for opportunities.*
* *is supportive.'*

Over time the relationship should develop to that of a dynamic duo.

He/she will be dignified with integrity and will demonstrate downward loyalty.

In terms of operating style, the person will be specific and organised in their instructions and will be demanding but not insensitive.

Résumé of

GRAHAM BOWER

15 Abbotsford Road, Homebush 2140

Tel: (02) 9637 3193

OBJECTIVE

To pursue my chosen career in Marketing with a preference for commercial objectives involving advertising and product promotion

RECORD OF RESPECTED EMPLOYERS

GEORGE SAMUELSON & PARTNERS PTY LTD

(Publishing & Conventions - Financial Market)   1996 — 1998

SAMPLE OF ACHIEVEMENTS

* *Marketing Co-ordination*

Served as liaison between travel services, hotels and convention managers to streamline many national food and retail conventions

Designed speaker profiles for conference programs

Negotiated and arranged with overseas speakers for accommodation, travel, presentations and speaker fees for three conventions

Streamlined directories for updating, selling and increasing the database for future systems

Organised press releases for up and coming events, printing of letters, programs, directories and publications.

* *Key Account Management*

Managed staff and outside contractors in many promotional campaigns, conferences and office duties

Answered customer inquiries and developed a large personal customer base

Liaised with subscription managers, writers, designers, desktop publishers and printers on all aspects of promotional campaign materials

* *Client Data Management*

Conducted updating systems for client database and two substantial business directory publications

Maintained a database for future campaigns and kept record of performance on database lists (10,000 records)

Key member in converting manual directory procedures to a highly sophisticated user friendly computerised system

Coordinated time schedules, flights, hotels and convention rooms for three conferences

Tracked internal and external database lists from direct mail campaigns and conference programs

* *Sales Management*

Worked on multiple projects simultaneously in highly pressured situations and consistently met strict deadline schedules

Telemarketed from database for the selling of goods and services

Increased subscriber entries for two national directories

Sold advertising space for two business directories and conference materials

Negotiated sponsorship for three conferences ($50,000 plus revenue)

Sold exhibition space for three conferences ($40,000 revenue)

EDUCATION

Completed Marketing Certificate at ADMA
Completed 1st year of Electrical Trade Certificate at TAFE
Completed HSC 1992 Pennant Hills Grammar School

MORE FACTS ABOUT ME

Recently travelled extensively through Europe over two month period and gained experience in travel, cultures and languages.

Prior to employment with George Samuelson, pursued an Apprenticeship in Electrical Trades over three year period carrying out promotion of services and subcontract work. Recession caused me to reassess my career direction.

Sailed in the 52nd anniversary Sydney to Hobart Race and many inshore season races.

PEOPLE WHO KNOW MY WORK WELL

Jerry Day
Editor in Chief
George Samuelson & Partners Pty Ltd
Tel: 9423 3922 (b)

Pat Watson
National Retail Manager
Upfront Australia
Tel: 9226 1999 (b)

Career Credentials of:

BARRY ROBERTSON

139 Edith Crescent, Balmoral Qld 4171
Contact data: 07 3319 4921 or 0412 392 102 or 07 3910 8839

EMPLOYMENT ASPIRATIONS

To utilise twenty years successful and rewarding commercial experience to obtain a General Management role within a Hospitality and/or Resort Environment where a major improvement in planning expertise, ROI, image and reputation is needed.

KEY AREAS OF KNOWLEDGE

Business Management
* Recruitment and Training
* Financial Management and Reporting
* Marketing Strategies
* Purchasing Negotiations
* Administrative Procedures and Control Systems

Hospitality
* Promotional Campaigns
* Client Satisfaction Monitoring
* Quality Volume Food and Beverage Management
* Small, Medium and Large Scale Operations

COMPREHENSIVE BUSINESS ORIENTATED EDUCATION

Ryde Technical College
Successfully completed two years Hotel and Catering Management

Graduated in Import and Export from Australian Institute of Import and Export Management following two years study

Completed a number of industry-specific training courses, such as Train-the-Trainer, Wine Appreciation, etc. both within employment environments and by personal investment in my professional development.

PROFESSIONAL ACHIEVEMENT RECORD

Skilled in People Management

Fifteen years of recruiting, training, motivating, controlling staff in most aspects of hotel, food and beverage service delivery

Achieved many productivity improvements by reforming communication systems and attitudes among staff of wide ethnic diversity

Negotiated workforce incentive program and workplace enterprise agreement incorporating profit share and 50 employees

Hospitality Establishment Growth

Initiated export earnings project concerning food products which involved negotiations with Indian Government officials and facilitating joint venture partner involvement

Contributed on request and commissions from Architects to advise on back of house staff and storage and traffic flow facilities in both pre-building and in reconstruction project situations

CAREER PATH RECORD

Initially learned my trade in high quality Restaurants and Hotels in Metropolitan Centres and resort areas including the Hotel InterContinental Sydney over ten year period, then drew on my entrepreneurial inclinations to build up a series of Hospitality and Food service operations in a Partner capacity reporting directly to absentee owner/investor.

I would highlight a special learning and challenging experience was to act in Receivership Appointed capacity to turn around a significant Gold Coast hotel.

While I am dedicated to customer / client satisfaction, growth and repeat business, my approach essentially incorporates such achievement within a profitable framework.

PEOPLE WHO KNOW MY WORK WELL

These will be supplied readily when appointment exploration has progressed further.

MORE FACTS ABOUT ME

Gained much from experience overseas in Paris carrying out all major functions within a prominent boutique hotel during 1983.

Australian citizen ... proud father of one and happily married.

Résumé of

RICHARD BOLTON

43 James Street   Email: rbolton@wanet.com.au
Midlands 6139   Tel/Fax: 9247 1132 (H)

OBJECTIVE

To obtain part time or freelance work in the field of publishing. To offer a wide range of experience in all types of print media, particularly consumer and professional magazines and newspapers.

KEY CHARACTERISTICS

FLEXIBILITY   **RELIABILITY**   **ENERGY**   **EXPERIENCE**

Flexibility is shown by my success in most areas of publishing—print production, page layout, electronic design and pagination, sub-editing, editing. To achieve these ends undertook training in:
Macintosh—Microsoft Word, QuarkXPress.
PC—Lotus Smart Suite, Windows 95.

Reliability is demonstrated by having worked to deadlines ranging between daily and one year.
In one part of my career—as chief sub-editor of the Sunday Westralian—did not miss one deadline in four and a half years. Have both the computer equipment/programs, aptitude and resiliency to work from home if that is required.

Energy is a trademark. At present I am fitting out a yacht, researching for a book on a navigator/explorer, tutoring students in navigation and acting as a director of a sailing club. My first loves, though, are words and publishing.

Experience has come through working with organisations such as News Limited, Melbourne Herald Group and Consolidated Press, as well as for myself and as a consultant.
Have worked in rotogravure, letterpress and offset.

CAREER HIGHLIGHTS

✔ Designed, edited and launched Open Gardening magazine in Australia. First edition sold 40,000 copies.

✔ Managed whole publication process of a group of trade and professional magazines—on time and to budget—for architects and for the music industry.

✔ While at the Westralian was production editor of Team magazine during its conception, design and successful launch. Was responsible for liaison between editorial, designers, graphic artists and printers.

✔ Wrote a yachting book for Thomson Publications. This has sold 30,000 copies and is in its second edition in Australia and North America.

EMPLOYMENT RECORD

News Limited	5 years
Self-employed	9 years
Melbourne Herald Group	15 years
Consolidated Press Ltd	6 years

BRUCE CHILDS

Tel: (02) 9499 3911 (W) or (02) 9818 1397 (H)
email: bruce.c@ozemail.com.au
28 Minchin Street, West Ryde 2114

OBJECTIVE

To work with a company where I can continue to make a positive contribution at a senior level which includes results accountability by involvement in corporate strategic planning, operations review and audit and financial planning.

PROFESSIONAL QUALIFICATIONS & STUDIES

Qualifications

- **Diploma in Corporate Management** (Dip. C.M.), Institute of Chartered Secretaries and Administrators (course designed by the Australian Graduate School of Management, University of New South Wales) 1997
- **Diploma** (with an "A" average), International Accountants Society, USA, 1983
- **Bachelor of Arts** (Sociology major), California State University, USA, 1988

Additional Studies

- Problem Solving and Decision Making, Kepner-Tregoe
- Interactive Management, Development Dimensions Intervention
- Export Procedures, Australian Institute of Export
- Accounting for Planning and Control for Not-for-Profit Organisations, National Association of Accountants, USA

SAMPLE OF ACHIEVEMENTS

1. Saved $2.0m on the purchase and installation of a $9.5m packaging equipment project
2. Developed unique spreadsheets to measure efficiently and effectively raw material utilisation, taking into account both theoretical capability and operating standards
3. Mechanised the budgeting process of a $55m budget for both overhead spending and direct / indirect labour
4. Key contributor in team which regained control of a $100m project by instigating meaningful site meetings, accurate projection of final costs, control of work scope, with tight control of commitments and expenditures
5. Headed negotiating team on what was considered a major unworkable contract, which developed strategies, coordinating and liaising with management, legal advisers and military client at the very highest levels of command, resolving the contract to a workable agreement enabling the company to fulfil its obligations

PROFESSIONAL EXPERIENCE

1995   **FREELANCE Consultant** — Projects included:
- 1998

CALCULATE PTY LTD
Developed accounting records, lease property schedules, filing systems, creditor rationale and liquidated all liabilities during 90 day shutdown

VIDEO FILMS
Developed gearing and accounting records, improved capital requirements, implemented computer system, produced balance sheets, profit and loss statements, cash flow projections

LIFE INSURANCE CO
Researched, designed and presented a National Superannuation Scheme for the Construction Industry Trade Unions of which we were a finalist

ELECTRONICS FIRM
Liaison between senior management and company solicitors, analysing complex company / Commonwealth contract legal issues, and negotiating strategies to a win / win result

1988   **CURTIN (AUSTRALIA) PTY LTD**
- 1995   Sales of $200m+ and over 900 employees

2 years   **Plant control managerial** responsibilities:
- Raw materials utilisation
- Labour rate efficiencies
- Indirect and direct labour hours
- Quarterly budgets
- Capital projects ($1m+)
  - justification, qualitative and quantitative, rates of return, IRR and NPV
- Costing union negotiation package

5 years   **Project Cost Controller** reporting to the Finance Director
Accountable for the total financial integrity of all capital projects. Capital spending was $100m+
- Interpretation of corporate directives into local policies and procedures
- Coordination of all aspects of financial capital planning and control
- Developing and implementing PC and Mainframe computerisation capital costs control system
- Purchase and implementation of fixed asset register (COFAS)
- Internal and external capital expenditure reports
- Coordination and liaison with project and industrial engineering, Director of Finance, Managing Director and USA parent company

1985   **LEGAL AID SOCIETY OF ORANGE COUNTY, USA**
- 1988   **Fiscal Officer** responsible for accounting unit, advising on financial records, analysis and forecasting, designed procurement records controlling cost and accountability. Major participant in allocation of resources and setting objectives / goals fund negotiating

1984   **PASCO PACIFIC CORPORATION**, (Division of Gulf & Western)
Transistor and other electrical configuration manufacturers — **Cost Accountant**

Résumé of:

VICKIE TARBIS

Unit 39, 36 Marbella Street
Sandy Bay 7005

Email: vickiet@sunrise.com.au
Tel: H (03) 6243 1235

CREDENTIALS FOR TASKS WHICH
UTILISE MY SKILLS AND ENTHUSIASM PREFERABLY ON A
PART-TIME, SUBCONTRACT, PROJECT OR JOB SHARE BASIS

PUBLICATION SKILL

- Designed, developed concept and made happen a regular issue Newsletter reaching 2000 and learnt how to research, write, edit, lay-out and oversee publication and mailing
- Publication of articles and essays in nationally distributed print media
- Mastered Publisher and Word in producing the publication
- Own Power Macintosh in daily use

ORGANISATIONAL FLAIR

- Initiated and organised many events, such as a national lecture tour by an overseas expert (35 presentations in 17 days), plus other seminars and tours
- Initiated and built a new concept of self-help service for impaired people, now with membership extending nationally
- Led many meetings of participants in self-help groups

COMMUNICATIONS ABILITY

- Presented many speeches in various public forums for the human care cause in the past two years
- Former Primary and Junior Schoolteacher for 15 years

CREATIVE

- Gained much from developing personal skill at creative presentation of magazine material

TENACITY

- Achieved some success in the difficult task of fund raising
- Am surviving well my undergraduate studies by correspondence on a part-time basis for BA from University of Queensland, having previously completed Teachers Certificate and Chemistry Certificate in earlier years, also Diploma of Freelance Journalism (1997)

PERSONAL

Have emerged stronger from personal transition in overcoming physical limitation. Now eager to expand skills, take on new projects and contribute to others in a practical way

RÉSUMÉ OF

PATRICIA HANDLEY

156 Edwards Street   Tel: (02) 6382 1732
Young 2594   or (02) 6383 1394

CREDENTIALS FOR APPOINTMENT TO THE STAFF OF
YOUNG AND DISTRICT HOSPITAL

OBJECTIVE

To be engaged in tasks associated with human care, counselling support and the education process involved in such activities.

My preference is for community service in a country-based environment where my extensive metropolitan and overseas experiences can be applied as appropriate. I am interested in either a full-time, part-time or job-sharing arrangement. Level of pay and hours of work are less important than the nature of problems to be solved.

CAREER SUMMARY

My employment experiences have ranged from secretarial and administrative tasks through to partnership in self-employment endeavours, during the course of which I raised three children. I am no stranger to working hard and being the custodian of confidential information. Recently have developed computer-usage competencies and considerable 'hands-on' experience using word processing, graphic design and spreadsheet software.

Former employment experiences have included work in Malta and England and in contrasting situations such as international conferences, building construction and photographic supplies. Among other skills developed, I am a competent administrator, used to negotiating and maintain a sense of humour in tense and difficult situations. Crisis management brings out the best in me.

SKILLS & KNOWLEDGE ENHANCEMENTS

- Welfare Work Certificate, Gymea College of TAFE, 1986-1989.
  Completed course with Honours Award through part-time studies and earned in the process several A and B Grade passes.

- Secretarial training in Brisbane.

PROFESSIONAL RECORD

- Completed nine months voluntary service with Wayside Chapel, Kings Cross, Sydney, engaged predominantly in crisis counselling people of all ages and socio-economic backgrounds. Understudied Social and Welfare Workers on home visits and in their discussion groups within the Life Education program.

- During studies developed awareness of, and contact information for, a wide range of community services for social and health problems with which I was involved. Liaised with other professional services when required.

- Participated in in-ward consultation program within St Vincent's Hospital, Darlinghurst helping others cope with adversity, bereavement, family and domestic issues, etc. Case report writing was a significant feature of this activity. Earned A Grade pass for field work.

PERSONAL DATA

Hold current Drivers Licence and fortunately a 20 year accident free record ..... Resident of Young District for 18 months ..... Energetic by nature ..... Permanent resident since 1984 ..... Referees will be provided when required.

RICKY KATZ

39/194 Hastings Street, Auchenflower 4066
Tel: (07) 3481 1394

OBJECTIVE

A management role where my ability in financial analysis, credit management, commercial evaluation and experience in diverse business environments will add value to the process of my employer achieving their goals.

CAREER SUMMARY

Over the past eight years I have gained extensive experience in the analysis of business viability and profitability. At the same time my role has included liaising and negotiating with clients. It is now my desire to apply this experience in a broader context, as part of a management team, in a challenging and stimulating environment.

MAIN CAPABILITIES

- In-depth business analysis

- Building positive relationships inter-company and externally

- Credit law

- Communication, orally and written

- Coordination of activities and staff

- Research, analysis and proposal development

PROFESSIONAL EMPLOYMENT

Slade Finance Ltd   March 1997 - April 1998

- Supervision of credit analysts

- Acceptance of new lease and loan recommendations (with an approval limit of $150,000)

- Financial analysis of proposals

- Supervision of major joint venture, real estate development

- Submission of financial proposals to Board level

- Maintaining close liaison with Finance Brokers

Manufacturers Kinghorn Aust. Ltd   July 1995 - March 1997

- Formulating credit recommendations for loan and trading facilities proposed by marketing staff

- Monthly reporting to US Head Office of facilities brought on board

- Reviewing performance of on-going trading facilities for Australian Top-500 corporations

- Supervision of repayment and draw down of loan facilities

PROFESSIONAL EMPLOYMENT continued

Craigiburn Finance Ltd   June 1991 - July 1995

- Analysis of leasing and loan proposals
- Supervision of junior analysts on day to day basis
- Close liaison with Finance Broker network
- Expansion of client base through direct marketing
- Vetting all ancillary documents pertinent to a facility to ensure company's interests
- Negotiation and structuring of terms in individual contracts
- Budgeting and forward planning
- Formulating recommendations to senior management and Board level
- Preparation of monthly reports to management and Statutory bodies
- Researching new areas of involvement
- Acting as liaison with valuers, solicitors, etc. as necessary prior to implementing a facility
- Ensure compliance with terms of facility and prepare all documentation for draw down
- Streamlining of approvals and settlements procedures by formulating checklists to be followed

PREVIOUS EMPLOYMENT

Prior employment was with several companies where responsibilities included credit appraisal and formulation of recommendations. My career commenced in the collections and recoveries area, with a range of experience in the agricultural and transport sectors during the recessionary period. Later I was also strongly involved with the financial appraisal of a dealer network and monitoring of their monthly accounts and floor-plan limits, as well as with conducting regular proof-checks at dealer locations.

FORMAL QUALIFICATIONS

- Master of Commerce (Accounting), University of Queensland. (This course, to be completed next year, satisfies academic requirements for Associate membership of the Australian Society of Accountants.) Achieved to date 1 Distinction, 5 Credits and 1 Pass.
- Bachelor of Arts (Economics and Econometrics), University of New South Wales
- Certificate in Pascal Programming, Queensland Institute of Technology
- Also completed four subjects towards an MBA, Institute of Administrators

OTHER COURSES

Extensive leadership and instructional technique training while in the Army Reserve over a five year period

SELWYN SHAPIRO

59 Penhurst Street, Leabrook 5068   Tel: (08) 8843 1325

OBJECTIVE

To contribute to the Marketing function in tasks associated with Market Research activities. Employment in either a full-time, part-time or freelance capacity would be acceptable.

MAIN KNOWLEDGE AREAS

- Market Research Interviewing - Consumer and Industrial
- Market Research - Domestic and Overseas
- Customer Liaison - Domestic and Overseas
- Sales Data Analysis
- Forecasting and Budgeting
- Commodity Trading and Pricing
- Computer Graphics
- Metals and Minerals Sales and Trading
- Field and Shipping Administration
- Purchasing and Raw Materials Negotiations

QUALIFICATIONS

Graduate Diploma in Marketing, University of South Australia (current part-time student in final year)
Member, Australian Institute of Materials Handling since 1985
Bachelor of Science, University of Melbourne, 1984

CURRENT ACTIVITIES

Market Research interview assignments both consumer and industrial for Horan Wall & Walker, plus gained valuable experience in the direct supervision of a major survey on behalf of the Urban Transit Authority.

PAST EMPLOYER

Employed by Alpha Petroleum & Minerals Limited for 14 years. Initial experience in supervision of manufacture and storage; followed by administration of warehousing and distribution of building materials; market research, forecasting, technical service and sales administration for minerals market research, bauxite alumina and aluminium contract administration.
My most recent position was Marketing Officer - Minerals.

CAREER RECORD

- Managed an effective aluminium, alumina and bauxite market and commercial intelligence system.

- Conducted and completed market surveys, price surveys and industry assessments on the above.

- Achieved through negotiated agreements with bauxite and aluminium customers contract price increases higher than CPI.

- Established valuable relationships with consultant analysts and personnel of industry associations.

- Monitored international iron ore, steel, silver, platinum, diamond, high technology minerals and markets.

- Managed the sales activities of products throughout South Australia.

- Completed nationwide market research of food and beverage industries that use sugar, nutrition issues, competitive products.

- Prepared forecasts of consumer consumption allowing for seasonal factors.

- Monitored costs and negotiated 10% reduction in rates for storage and transport of materials.

- Designed layouts and advised on bulk storage of materials.

- Supervised 24 chemical staff, laboratory personnel, manufacture and storage.

PERSONAL

- Studying for Graduate Diploma in Marketing at University of South Australia. Successfully completed first year gaining credits in Marketing Theory and Practice. Currently studying Marketing Research and Multinational Marketing.

- Previously active member, Apex Club. During seven year membership period held the positions of Social and Membership Director, Treasurer and Secretary.

MELODY AUGUSTIN

7 Etherington Street, Nedlands 6006
Tel: (08) 9487 9421 (home)

CAREER OBJECTIVE

To be engaged in sub-contract, casual or part-time employment in Market Research activities where my research and information analysis skills, coupled with my formal training in my degree studies in Psychology can be usefully applied. Have a preference for projects which examine social, community and behavioural issues.

BACKGROUND TO CAREER OBJECTIVE

- Gained particular knowledge and genuine interest in social and community issues during my university training. I studied issues in Comparative Sociology, Sociology of Development and City, State and Class, Behavioural Sciences and Developmental and Social Psychology

- My past employment has contributed to a knowledge of diverse industries, products and services and included, for example, real estate, insurance, pharmaceuticals, computers, advertising and community service

TERTIARY QUALIFICATIONS

Bachelor of Arts degree from Curtin University, majoring in Psychology—Graduated in 1995 following six years part-time study. Achieved several A and B subject grades and particularly gained much from studies in Sociology, Behavioural Sciences, Demography, Group Processes, Motivation, Research Design and Statistics for Social Sciences

PROFESSIONAL DEVELOPMENT COURSES

- Volunteer Training Program, covering communication skills and welfare service provision with the Lone Parent Family Resource Centre

- Conflict Resolution course conducted by Conflict Resolution Network

- Transformation (Personal Growth and Awareness) Courses

- Marriage and Family Counselling Training, conducted by Unifam (12 month course)

- Transactional Analysis course

ORGANISATION AND PLANNING ABILITY

- Researched and collated material used for 24 newspaper articles

- Developed project planning skills when conducting telephone surveys and door-to-door interviews

- Well developed library and internet research skills including use of computer-based information systems

RESEARCH, WRITING AND ANALYTICAL SKILLS

- Interviewed in-depth, middle and upper management of selected WA manufacturing companies to establish demand for training schemes for all levels of the workforce, particularly the shop floor staff. This was on behalf of the Advanced Manufacturing Centre

- Researched stories for media use and assisted in the writing of press releases

- Developed greater understanding of professional techniques necessary to target media coverage by attending a Journalistic publicity course at Nedlands Evening College

SOCIAL RESEARCH ACTIVITIES

- Capable in qualitative and quantitative research, data analysis, group interviews, report writing, fieldwork, and behaviour and motivation descriptions

- Addressed large groups of children and their teachers in relation to the complex issue of Multiple Sclerosis

- Communicated the objectives of a disadvantaged group in our community

- Discussed, communicated ideas, objectives, information and content to committee members, administration and project coordinator for the Nedlands project

LIAISON SKILLS

- Consulted numerous ethnic community groups, support agencies and experts in the field to review cogently the immediate problems associated with people from non-English speaking backgrounds

- Supported a human care activity by acting as an intermediary and coordinator for the Multiple Sclerosis Society's Read-a-thon program

- Selected as media team member for ocean yacht race by Fremantle Yacht Club

CAREER RECORD

Nedlands Community Services   **1996-98**
Project Officer

ABC Market Research Group   **1996**
Interviewer

Computer Management Services   **1995**
Assistant to Accountant and Company Secretary

Part-Time/Temporary Positions   **1989-93**
Utilising communication skills, working with clients, patients and the general public

Prior to the birth of my son, I acquired valuable administrative report writing and general public liaison experience working in several industries.

Résumé of:

DAVID DEWAR

141 Edwards Street	Tel: (h) 02 9389 3192
Bronte 2024	or leave message 02 9410 2367

OBJECTIVE

To apply twenty years' marketing, product development and commercial management experience to a private sector organisation selling product lines to other businesses.

LOCATION

Sydney, preferably light industry, medium or large organisation with revenue generation responsibility up to $80m

PRECIS OF COMPETENCIES

MARKETING TO PRIVATE SECTOR
MARKETING TO PUBLIC SECTOR
FORECASTING, BUDGET PLANNING AND CONTROL
PRODUCT DEVELOPMENT
SALES FORCE MANAGEMENT
STAFF RECRUITMENT, MOTIVATION AND DEVELOPMENT
ACQUISITION NEGOTIATIONS
DISTRIBUTION
POST SALES SERVICE

CAREER RECORD

Media Aids Pty Ltd	**1976 to 1998**
General Manager, Business and Visual Products	1991 - 1998
Assistant Manager, Audio Visual Division	1981 - 1991
Sales Representative	1979 - 1981
Management Trainee	1976 - 1979

CAREER SUMMARY

Initially engaged as a trainee, my employment has been continuously with Media Aids Pty Ltd. Early assignments included learning roles in Accounts, Payroll, Manufacturing, Consumer Products and Industrial Products, before being appointed to sell throughout New South Wales. Advancement to management responsibilities was earned in 1982. Increasing accountability occurred over the following years with formal involvement as Associate Director in total company operations in 1995, while continuing with executive management responsibilities for the Business and Visual Products Division.

PROFESSIONAL DEVELOPMENT

Participated in many seminars and workshops in such subject areas as salesmanship, "Masters of Success", Leadership, Effective Management, One Minute management and completed two Certificates (TAFE) in Management and Supervision through part-time studies

EXAMPLES OF COMMERCIAL ACHIEVEMENTS

- Provided major input to development of Division Strategic Plan

- Researched, identified and evaluated synergistic acquisition possibilities with potential to increase revenue by 70%

- Directed the development of national advertising and promotional campaigns and materials, the majority produced in-house

- Since 1996 managed to double Divisional sales volume while maintaining margins

- Regularly travelled overseas to source new products, with special attention to North American developments

- Doubled net profit consistently over three years

- Won NSW Public Sector contract in 1993 and retained since then against strong competition

- Successful in proposal to supply film to major processing laboratory — annual revenue contribution of $1m

- Successfully expanded internationally, with major successes being in New Zealand market. Most notable success being winning and retaining Government contract for past eight years

- Active contributor to business improvement analysis consultancy project provided by Ernst & Young

REFERENCES AVAILABLE ON REQUEST

Career Profile of:

MEGAN BEARDSLEY

COMMUNICATION TRAINING CONSULTANT

SOUND CREDENTIALS AND EXPERIENCE FOR EVALUATING AND ENHANCING ALL ASPECTS OF PERSONAL COMMUNICATION

PROFESSIONAL QUALIFICATIONS

Licentiateship, College of Speech Therapy, London, 1990
Member, Australian Association of Speech & Hearing (MAASH)

CONTACT INFORMATION

Address:
1/16 Illiliwa Street
Fortitude Valley 4006

Telephone:
Home (07) 3953 9253
Work (07) 3969 4393

RANGE OF SERVICES

Seminar / Workshop Presentations that provide professional informative, up-to-date tuition based on the particular communicative needs of the participants

Individual Consultations which include individual evaluation and training sessions to enhance and improve the participant's communication and interpersonal skills

TRAINING PROVIDED

Speech
- Physiology of speech production
- Voice analysis — individual
- Voice projection and optimal use of breathing
- Maintenance of a good, strong speaking voice
- General elocution
- Accent refinement
- Assessment and remediation of specific difficulties, e.g. stuttering

Language
- Teaching and refinement of grammar and language usage
- Improvement of understanding of English, including methods to increase retention of information

Communication
- Public speaking
- Interviewing techniques
- Interpersonal skills
- Active listening
- Non-verbal communication
- Self-evaluation and refinement of overall communication skills

PROFESSIONAL BACKGROUND

- Speech pathologist with seven years' experience in both the public and private sectors

- Experience in tertiary level student supervision, lecturing and teaching English as a foreign language to both individuals and groups

- Acted as a Speech Pathology Consultant within many educational environments

- My interests continue to be in people and how they communicate — areas in which I have amassed considerable knowledge and practical experience. Have participated in many workshops in counselling, middle management skills and learning difficulties in individuals

Career Summary and Résumé
of

ALAN DIXON

---

25 Camellia Crescent, Ormiston 4160   Telephone: (07) 8381.3973

OBJECTIVE:

- To be employed either in Brisbane, South East Asia or the Pacific Region where commercial development and marketing problems need to be solved.

- To use management, marketing, purchasing and international trading skills in an employment environment where my experience can be applied to improve trading results and relations with distributors and customers.

MAIN KNOWLEDGE AREAS:

- Merchandising
- Export Sales
- Share Market Trading
- International Trading
- Budgeting, Forecasts and Cost Control
- Food and Beverages Processing

- Product Development
- Retail Trading
- Commodity Trading
- Property Sales
- Major Account Negotiations
- Distribution and Warehousing

CAREER SUMMARY:

My commercial skills have been developed and applied in a number of industry sectors. The major one has been **Food and Beverages Processing** where I have had production, marketing and branch management experience.

Products with which I have been associated include, for example, soft drinks, confectionery, pharmaceuticals, banking, milk products, together with an extensive knowledge of sports equipment, clothing and footwear.

I have substantial experience managing and trading in many countries in South East Asia.

TERTIARY EDUCATION:	Completed a Diploma in Dairy Manufacture and Food Technology with 2nd Class Honours at the commencement of my career.
PAST EMPLOYERS:	These have included a sporting goods retailer (7 years), manufacturer and marketing firm in food flavours and essences, F H Faulding (6 years), Cold Storage Holdings —Creameries Division in Singapore and Malaysia (9 years) and Peters Ice Cream and Milk (5 years).
	Position titles have been Assistant Production Manager, Branch Manager, Manager Export Division, Commercial Development Manager.
PERSONAL:	Currently a resident of Brisbane but prepared to relocate overseas subject to nature of career opportunity.
	Take an active interest in Rugby Union, as both a Coach (Advanced Coaching Certificate) and Administrator (past Director and Treasurer, South Brisbane Rugby Club).
	'A' Grade golfer. Enjoy excellent health and maintain personal fitness program.

COMPREHENSIVE REFERENCES AVAILABLE ON REQUEST

Résumé of:

GEORGE HAZELRIGG

SOUND CREDENTIALS AND EXPERIENCE FOR EVALUATING AND ENHANCING ALL ASPECTS OF SPORTS MEDICINE AND HEALTH MANAGEMENT

PROFESSIONAL QUALIFICATIONS

- Member, Australian Physiotherapy Association
- BAppSc (Physiotherapy) Graduated from Cumberland College of Health Sciences 1994
- Undergraduate studies in BAppSc (Occupational Therapy) and within the BSc syllabus (University of Sydney)

CONTACT INFORMATION

Address:
PO Box 246
Cremorne 2090

Telephone:
(02) 9908.6037

George Hazelrigg   **Page 2**

PRECIS OF COMPETENCIES

Diagnosis, Treatment and Prevention of sports injuries and non-sports injuries

Fitness Assessment of sedentary individuals and both intermediate and elite athletes

Biomechanical Analysis

Post Operative, Intensive Care & General Outpatient Physiotherapy

Clinical activities covering such areas as Sports Surgery, Orthopaedics, Spinal Disorders, Paediatrics, Neurology, Cardiothoracics, Chronic Pain, etc.

Health and Lifestyle Counselling and Program Design

PROFESSIONAL BACKGROUND

Either through employment, special study projects or self-initiated research, I have been involved in the activities of a range of human care environments including hospitals, sports clinics, surgical, general practice and laboratories. Such institutions have included The Sports Clinic (NSW Sports Science & Research Centre) at Cumberland College, Australian Institute of Sport, Australian Rules Football Club, Baulkham Hills Private Hospital, Westmead, Lidcombe and Royal Prince Alfred Hospitals, Camperdown Children's Hospital, St George Institute of Education and several High Schools.

OTHER FACTS ABOUT ME

Experienced as a Lecturer, Writer of Articles, Demonstrator and Counsellor

PEOPLE WHO KNOW MY WORK WELL

Dean Faculty of Nursing & Community Studies
Mrs M Telford
University of Western Sydney
Tel: (02) 4570 1400 (W)

Orthopaedic Surgeon
Dr S Burton
Orthopaedic & Sports Medicine Centre
Tel: (02) 9437 2411 (W)

Professional Profile of:

STEPHANIE SENTURIA

Email: ssenturia@bigpond.com.au

Telephone: (02) 9370 7311

CAREER OBJECTIVE

To develop innovative and quality radio programs and contribute to broadcasting policy by applying my creative, technical and research skills.

PROFESSIONAL EXPERIENCE AND CAPABILITIES

Radio Production:

- Four years' hands-on experience in interviewing, editing, presentation and production at the national broadcasting organisation, the Australian Broadcasting Corporation (ABC) and at the public broadcasting station, 2CBA-FM.

- Researcher, production secretary and music coordinator for Drive Time, on ABC Radio.

- Producer of several radio series based on Australian children's fiction, broadcast on ABC Radio.

- Producer and presenter at 2CBA-FM of Lifeskills Program, a two-hour weekly live program. Also regular contributor to Consumer Hints and The Arts Diary.

Research and Writing:

- Four years' experience in research and writing for short-term and long-term projects, as well as managing well the usual emergencies that arise in live broadcasting.

- Senior Research Officer for 15 months at the Australian Broadcasting Tribunal, the licensing and regulatory authority for commercial and public broadcasting. Employed on the Special Projects Inquiry into Remote Commercial Television Services, Australia's first commercial television service to broadcast via AUSSAT. Responsible for research, compilation and analyses of financial and marketing issues for the First Report. Responsible for coordinating other officers for the Second and Third Reports.

- Researcher for a daily current affairs program at the ABC, a weekly program at 2CBA-FM and a two-part feature for ABC Radio. Prepared scripts and interview questions.

PROFESSIONAL EXPERIENCE AND CAPABILITIES continued

Management and Administration:

- Responsible for the administration and coordination of two Inquiries and Reports for the Australian Broadcasting Tribunal. Responsible for correspondence, dealing with confidential financial information and custody of the file of the Inquiry.

- Member of the Volunteers Committee at 2CBA-FM and the Volunteer Representative on the Management Committee.

Script Assessment:

- Two years' experience as a freelance script editor for the Radio Drama Department, ABC. Read and assessed scripts from Australia, Britain, Ireland, Germany, Hungary and Poland for possible production. Wrote detailed and critical reports on the scripts.

Musicianship:

- Studied flute at the New South Wales Conservatorium of Music. Australian Music Examinations Board - Honours in 7th Grade Practical, Credit in 5th Grade Musicianship.

- Flute teacher for three years. Studied piano for four years.

TERTIARY EDUCATION

Bachelor of Arts in Communications.
University of Technology, Sydney, 1989-1991
Majors: Radio Production
             Professional Writing
             Literary Studies

Community Theatre Arts Course.
East Sydney College of TAFE — 1994

REFERENCES AVAILABLE ON REQUEST

Résumé of:

STEPHEN ERBER

39 Koala Crescent   Tel: (08) 8229.3411 (W)
Henley Beach 5022   (08) 8859.4307 (H)

CAREER OBJECTIVE

To apply my skills in financial planning, quantitative and qualitative analysis of investment opportunities and technical knowledge of legislation, economics, social security, taxation and various markets in a practical role with a well respected financial institution.

Keen to apply the above to enhance liaison with clients, the pursuit of excellence in the securities industry and the promotion of a range of high quality services.

CAREER SKILLS SUMMARY

- **INVESTMENT SERVICES ADVICE** — three years' experience as a personal financial management consultant, business development manager and senior financial planner with both a financial planning company and a stockbroking company. Noted success with sales effectiveness and client satisfaction and retention.

- **INVESTMENT ANALYSIS** — quantitative and qualitative analysis of listed and unlisted investment opportunities in fixed interest, cash, property and share markets. Enhanced by near completion of the Securities Industry course (now in final semester).

- **COMMUNICATION SKILLS** — previous 20 year successful career leading and managing as a Naval Officer; augmented by part-time teaching at TAFE College and a variety of other interests involving personal interaction. Particular expertise in arranging seminars and giving presentations.

- **PROBLEM SOLVING** — years of involvement in tactical planning and decision making has resulted in an ability to arrive at solutions quickly and pursue them to a logical conclusion.

- **ORGANISATIONAL AND MANAGEMENT** — very experienced in planning, organising and executing set goals. Am able to work effectively with professionals, liaise with organisations and coordinate and lead groups.

Stephen Erber   **Page 2**

QUALIFICATIONS

• Securities Institute Certificate (Final Semester)

• Dealers Representative Licence, 1996

• Australian Certified Investment Planner Certificate, 1996

• Financial Planners Introductory Course Certificate, 1995

EDUCATION

Management, Leadership and Technical training with the armed forces (details available on request)

Higher School Certificate, St George's High School, 1978

CAREER SUMMARY

1995 - 98	Financial Planner (including use of retirement, superannuation and other managed products) and Analyst, Thomas & Co Ltd
1994 - 95	Senior Directing Staff Officer, Naval Officers Warfare School
1992 - 94	Exchange duty with United States Navy
1990 - 92	Principal Staff Officer, Her Majesty's Australian Fleet HQ
1989	RAN Staff College: subjects included Quantitative Analysis (top student), Computer Programming, Problem-Solving Techniques
1987 - 89	Warship PERTH - Operations Officer. Selected Second in Command
1987	Training in the United Kingdom
1979 - 86	Various operational and staff positions, both ashore and at sea

OTHER PROFESSIONAL DEVELOPMENT

• South Australian Institute of Technology, one semester course in Statistics

• Part-time Teacher, Business Studies, Glenelg TAFE - 2 years

Résumé of:

DAVE SHIRLEY

Tel: (02) 9326.3985 (h)

Credentials for appointment within the Financial Services Industry sector either within Treasury activities or Corporate/Project Finance

---

OBJECTIVE

To apply my key skills in quantitative analysis, methodical approach, understanding of economics and problem-solving ability in a role where practical financial information is the outcome of my efforts. Am no stranger to liaison with clients, working to tight time schedules, devising mathematical formulae and engagement on complex problem-solving assignments involving research and analysis.

CREDENTIALS

Tertiary education accomplishments in a numerate discipline, stable employment record, recent and ongoing success in Securities Institute studies and a desire to re-align my career path by transferring my basic skills to a different industry following detailed career analysis and careful self-assessment of my occupational preferences.

RECORD OF CURRENT STUDIES

The Securities Institute of Australia Diploma
Successfully completed:
Australian Futures Trading - Distinction, Options Markets and Trading - Distinction, Security Industry Economics - Credit, Introduction to Investment Analysis - Credit, Introduction to the Securities Industry - Credit, Securities Industry Law - Pass; currently enrolled in Applied Corporate Finance and Applied Portfolio Management

TERTIARY EDUCATION

Master of Engineering Science Majoring in Structures
    Awarded 1991, University of Sydney
    Completed with mainly High Distinctions and Distinctions awarded

BSc, BEng (Civil) Honours Class 1
    Graduated 1989, University of Sydney
    Completed with mainly High Distinctions and Distinctions awarded

Normanhurst High School, 1980-81
    1st Place: Commerce (2 years) and Economics (2 years)

COMPUTER FAMILIARITY

Computer Programming during Undergraduate and Masters Degrees
Use of structural analysis packages during employment
Preparation of logic for structural analysis program during employment, some use of statistics
Programming languages: Basic, Fortran and Pascal

COMMUNICATION SKILLS

High standard of written communications developed through preparation of conference papers, project reports, client correspondence and presentation of quantitative data over past eight years

EMPLOYMENT RECORD

Stephenson Goodhall Pty Ltd
(Consulting Engineers)   **January 1990 to present**
Associate Director, Senior Design Engineer, Design Engineer

PERSONAL

Personal activities in the Stock Market for several years...Treasurer of Water Ski Club for several years...employment location preference is Sydney...Member Institution of Engineers since 1995...enjoy sporting activities, particularly touch football, and increasing my knowledge and acquisition of wines

29 Devondale Street, Woollahra 2025

WENDY HILL

127 Marbella Road
CARLTON 3053

Tel: h (03) 9953 4912
or b (03) 9261 7371

CREDENTIALS FOR APPOINTMENT TO THE POSITION OF
HUMAN RESOURCES TRAINING & DEVELOPMENT COORDINATOR

OBJECTIVE

To apply many years' experience training others and ten years in leadership in learning initiatives, management and staff training program design and provide high level interpersonal and communication skills to enhance the performance and employability of employees.

SUMMARY

My background is within varied learning and human development fields which has involved an understanding of the needs of the organisation and the needs of participants in the learning activities; the design and adaptation of training based on thoroughly researched principles of adult learning; designing, implementing and evaluating tuition has been a continuing component of my work while being promoted regularly to more senior responsibilities.

PROFESSIONAL QUALIFICATIONS

B.Ed. studies shortly to be completed; preceded by earlier studies for the Diploma in Teaching and the Trained Secondary Teachers Certificate (Toorak Teachers College and University of Melbourne)

Participated in over 30 professional development workshops and seminars, as well as State and National level conferences

EMPLOYMENT RECORD

VICTORIAN DEPARTMENT OF EDUCATION   **1984** TO PRESENT
Special Educational Consultant
Organisational change interventions ... Needs analyses ... Personal development counselling ... Written material for training resource manuals ... Special tuition constructs for drug & alcohol and behaviour management issues (Employee Assistance Programs) ... Interviewing training ... Training proposal and submissions to Executive management ... Cost justifications ... Tuition evaluation procedures ... Consultancy to Unit and Divisional Managers ... Diagnostic aids ... Timetable, training budget, resources allocation for training events ... Conference, workshop and seminar organisation and presentation ... Committee participation ... Published articles on Behaviour Management Techniques ... Morale audits ... Policy research, writing and implementation ... Identifying and evaluating external consultants and other specialist services ... Special programs for multicultural, computer and equal opportunity purposes ... Validating requests for training actions ... Measurement of learning effectiveness

VICTORIAN DEPARTMENT OF EDUCATION   **1973** TO **1983**
Trainee Teacher through to Deputy Principal

RÉSUMÉ OF:

WAYNE MORAN

58 Warburton Street   Tel: 9489.1347 (H)
Winthrop 6150   Message: 9381.3291

OBJECTIVE

To apply my marketing and sales management experience, together with successful tertiary studies, to the expansion of my employer's business in an efficient and profitable manner.

CAREER SUMMARY

My worklife experiences have included overseas appointments and substantial responsibilities for revenue and customer service. From these I have learned much and contributed energetically to achieving my employers' objectives. In particular, recent skills development has increased my awareness of complex product costing, profit optimisation and initiatives into new markets.

PERSONAL DEVELOPMENT AND QUALIFICATIONS

- Won selection for and successfully completed Curtin University (School of Marketing) Certificate Course in Marketing (1996)

- Completed studies part-time in Basic Marketing Certificate (West Perth College of TAFE). Completed QANTAS Export Procedures Training Course. Participated in Workshop 'Account Development Strategies' (Learning Systems International)

EMPLOYMENT RECORD

Cats Business Design and Marketing Pty Ltd   **August 1996 to date**
Responsible for the marketing, sales and product design functions, reporting to the Marketing Director.

Nature of Business:
- Design and manufacture of specialist exhibition presentations
- Interior design, shop-fitting, joinery
- Project management for tenancy fit-outs

Responsibilities:
- Research and develop new markets and plan and implement the launch of new products
- Supervise sales, technical and administrative staff
- Research and compile sales forecasts and budgets on new products and markets
- Maximise profitability by reducing overheads
- Prepare and maintain accurate job costings
- Develop packages and products in exhibition market sector

Cats Business Design and Marketing Pty Ltd continued

Accomplishments:
- Researched, evaluated and subsequently extended employer's business into two new market sectors
- Sourced tender information from major building industry groups which eventuated in winning contracts at Fremantle Exhibition Centre
- Generated 25% increase in turnover in Exhibition market in 12 months
- Negotiated on government and private sector tender contracts and maintained complete project management on design and manufacture budgets from $50,000 to $200,000
- Controlled Exhibition Market Sector with annual turnover ($2 million)

International Carriers Ltd   **June 1992 to July 1996**
(London, Bahrain, and Perth)

My first appointment was as **Credit Control Clerk**, later as **Sales Office Management** and **Sales Representation** in London office. I was selected for assignment to Bahrain initially as **Sales Representative**. Subsequently, further promotion to **Sales Manager** for the Bahrain Sales and Operations Office occurred in early 1995.

- Increased existing client revenue by 15% and accomplished 10% new business revenue in excess of budget target
- Honed negotiation skills in contract and tender marketing with Arab counterparts and Local Government Officials
- From date of assignment in new territory met revenue targets each month
- Launched two new products effectively after researching legal and financial aspects
- In highly competitive West End market of London accomplished major extension of public relations activities resulting in new business

Shell Australia Pty Ltd   **December 1989 to January 1992**

Sales Ledger Clerk: Liaised with clients and agents over rebates and account enquiries, and involved in accounting procedures such as invoicing, monthly reporting, sales tax administration, etc. As part of a retail sales training program, undertook part-time management of retail sites and at time of resignation was totally responsible for the property management, cash management and security, and stock control for a major Service Station.

OTHER FACTS

No stranger to adapting to new situations and working hard…particularly enjoy the intellectual challenges in marketing strategy development as well as their implementation…active sportsperson…referees will be provided if required.

Résumé of:

GARY EVANS

Tel: (03) 6260 3123 or leave message on (03) 6263 3015

OBJECTIVE

A research and advisory position within the environmental sciences where my tertiary training in earth and marine sciences and experiences within Australia and overseas can be applied to environmental issues

GEOGRAPHICAL COVERAGE

Assignments to date have included work within New South Wales, Queensland (and South Pacific Rim), Tasmania, Western Australia; North West Territories and Northern Saskatchewan, Canada; also South and North Island, New Zealand

PRECIS OF EXPERIENCE

Managing Environmental Studies:

Assisted in oil pollution toxicology studies on Sydney Rock and Pacific Oysters

Participated in and reported on University studies of Lady Musgrove Island on Great Barrier Reef. Also Sydney Harbour sedimentation, sonar interpretation and mini submarine surveys

Participated in studies of marine biology and sedimentation in Bass Strait

Technical:

Solved logistical and organisational problems in field camps—between contractors, management and staff

Compiled detailed maps from aerial photographs and ground exploration

Conducted oil exploration drilling on NW Shelf Western Australia

Consulted on soil erosion during Canadian summer for ski resort in British Columbia

Interaction with Industry and Government:

Acquired comprehensive knowledge of legislative requirements relevant to mineral extraction and exploration

Conducted lease acquisition and liaison with Lands Dept and Bureau of Mineral Resources

Liaised with operating mines concerning daily mining operations, mine rehabilitation and economic management

Self-funded tour of Alaskan oil spill and appraisals of interactions of parties involved, i.e. technical, media and officials

Negotiated with land owners and government officers at State and Federal level

Financial Management:

Monitored and reported on exploration project budgets

Organised and managed contractors and field staff payments

Supervisory:

Managed field camps of up to 14 staff over extended periods

Effectively liaised with Field Assistants and Company executives

Planned and supervised alluvial gold trial mining project

OTHER SKILLS DEVELOPMENT

Competed a number of training courses including such subjects as First Aid, Gold Exploration Sampling, Staff Supervision, Computer Skills.

EMPLOYMENT RECORD

Burkett Henderson Consulting Ltd Canada	4 months
Everton Explorations (Australia)/CSR Minerals	12 months
CRA Mining Ltd	13 months
Minenco Corporation	9 months
Halberton Overseas	4 months
Fairley Oil & Overward Mining	
Part-time employment concurrent with studies	

FORMAL QUALIFICATIONS

BSc Double Geology Major. Thomas Cook University, Graduated 1994

PROFESSIONAL MEMBERSHIPS

Australian Institute of Mining and Metallurgy
Thomas Cook Queensland Geological Society

OTHERS FACTS ABOUT ME

Prepared to travel at short notice ... Enjoy excellent health and fitness

CONTACT ADDRESS

32/204 Glebe Point Road, Shipwrights Point 7116

Career Profile of:

LORRAINE CONLON

Telephone: (08) 8413.3148 (H)
(08) 8411.3299 (W)
(Prepared to relocate subject to employment opportunity)
(Available for employment within two weeks of an appointment)

OBJECTIVE

To be employed in the Publishing Industry as an Editorial Staff Member, where my eight years of secondary education teaching experience of English and History and my love for and aptitude in the English language will be utilised and extended.

CAPABILITY SUMMARY

I am effective in working with groups of people in an initiatory and supervisory capacity and as a presenter of information to others. I can work independently or as part of a team. Have demonstrated an ability for design and implementation of concepts, time management and sound communication skills, both written and oral. Am able to organise and accept responsibility. Experience in copy production and printing processes has also been gained.

EDUCATION

BA, Majoring in English and History, University of Adelaide, 1988

Diploma of Education, University of Adelaide, 1989

PRECIS OF SKILLS

- Established the school magazine, 'Revelations' (100 pages, 550 copies)—an activity which involved many diverse skills, e.g. fundraising; budgeting and print run decision making; liaison with students, staff and the business community; selection and editing of magazine copy; photography: subject selection, processing and screening; layout; proofreading; marketing and sales administration

- Proven aptitude in critical analysis, design and basic editing skills

- Identifying problems and inefficient processes and suggesting and implementing solutions

- Design and production of training aids and resources, e.g. slides, overhead transparencies, videos, senior text notes

- Motivation of participants in the learning process

PRECIS OF SKILLS continued

- Ability to recognise, motivate and utilise the skills of 25 persons in the production of the school magazine

- Capable of adapting concepts to suit the needs and abilities of diverse groups

- Ability to communicate with a wide variety of people and establish trust and rapport in the working environment

- Ability to communicate effectively and concisely in written and oral form

EXAMPLES OF COMMUNICATIVE ABILITY

- Research, compilation and presentation of reports, programs, submissions, e.g. Student Liaison Officer PEP submission to the Education Department

- Devised and implemented policy changes designed to develop a more productive, positive work environment, e.g. Drop Everything And Read program (DEAR), examination policy and course content within the English faculty

- Experienced in achieving results through others by involvement in Adult Education. Served, in a voluntary capacity, as Secretary of the Community Studies Centre, McLaren Vale Region, (2 years); Committee Member, (3 years)

- Active involvement in programs designed to foster pupil and staff welfare, e.g. Peer Support and Participation and Equity Program

- Eight years' experience in planning programs and designing curriculum units

PERSONAL TRAITS

- Quick grasp of detail
- Perception
- Love of literature
- Sense of thoroughness and accuracy
- Adaptability
- Professionalism

PERSONAL DATA

Enjoy reading, theatre, scuba diving, travel, tennis, choral society

Address: 48 Cliff Street, McLaren Vale 5171

REFERENCES AND REFEREES AVAILABLE ON REQUEST

WILLIAM BUCKLEY

25 Martin Drive, Minjilang 0822   Tel: (08) 8928 3102 (H)

OBJECTIVE

To be employed in an Employee Development environment which rewards fairly by results achieved and which appreciates hard work and integrity in carrying out assigned tasks.

Am skilled in working with groups of people and am an effective presenter of data to others. I can work independently or fit in and work well within a team.

PROFESSIONAL SKILLS AND ACHIEVEMENTS

Training Skills

- Assessment of youth and adult learning needs

- Determining structure, content, suitability and application of tuition programs, resources, time and people

- Design and production of training aids and resources with a variety of audio-visual materials, and working with a range of media products involved in the production of media presentations

- Able to speak comfortably and effectively to small and large groups

Organisation and Planning Ability

- Developed the capacity to handle efficiently own workload and to organise others

- Coordinated participants in particular programs, functions and competitions

- Evaluated effectiveness of programs, time and people

- Organised the work tasks and schedules of others and the performance required

Administration

- Assistant Form Master of Years 9 and 10 requiring roll-keeping, communications with parents, counselling skills, organisation of sport

Communication Skills

- Provided information and instruction to other staff members and members of the public to increase their expertise or knowledge on a particular subject matter

- Presentation of documentation of programs, schedules, rationales and objectives

- Comfortable when in liaison with varied age groups, occupations and administrative levels

- Dealing with situation specific vocabularies—legal, business and educational

- Devised methods of promoting various events, both school-based and community

CAPABILITY SUMMARY

While the major part of my employment has occurred within the secondary education system, I have gained valuable experience as an instructor in the adult HSC course at the Darwin College of TAFE.

PROFESSIONAL DEVELOPMENT AND FORMAL TRAINING

- Currently undertaking Masters of Education (University of New England) as an external student

- BA (University of Sydney) 1992

- Diploma of Teaching (Catholic College of Education) 1986

CAREER RECORD

St John's College   **1990 to date**
English and History Teacher and Coordinator of Year 9 program for three years

Darwin College of TAFE   **1997 to date**
Concurrent with the above, part-time teacher of Modern History, including contribution to the Modern History Assessment Scheme

St Bartholomew's College   **1987 - 1989**
English and History Teacher, and Assistant Form Master Years 9 and 10

REFERENCES WILL BE PROVIDED ON REQUEST

FIONA RICHARDS

<u>Telephone: (07) 3543.1785</u>   <u>Email: f.richards@msn.com.au</u>

OBJECTIVE

To obtain a long-term position within the Hospitality and/or Tourism sector where my communications ability, training and skill in interpersonal relations and time management can be applied.

My competencies could be usefully engaged in tasks associated with customer and public relations, staff training and learning events administration.

Availability for employment: Immediate

SUMMARY OF SKILLS

My teacher training and practical experience over 14 years has developed competencies in dealing with difficult and challenging situations on a daily basis. Leading groups, organising the work of others and conflict resolution have resulted in my having an easy rapport with students, teacher colleagues, parents and other clients

EMPLOYMENT RECORD

Qld Department of Education   1984 to 1998

Initially appointed as an Assistant Teacher then promoted in turn to Executive Teacher with the concluding position being as Assistant Principal. Fulfilled temporary position as Pre-school Director on a number of occasions.

PROFESSIONAL EXPERIENCE

1. Communications

*   Dealing with customer inquiries while working for the State Bank (five months) and Fortitude Valley Community Centre (several periods over five years)

*   Experienced in speaking to small and large groups—students, parents, general public—concerning education, current affairs and community interests

*   Design of tuition programs, scheduling of training and evaluation methods for instruction and learning have featured regularly in my employment

PROFESSIONAL EXPERIENCE continued

2. Management

*   Administered budgets and funds allocation, plus expense control

*   Designing situations for staff development and their participation in the decision-making process

3. Organisation

*   Assessments of learning needs

*   Determining structure, content, suitability and application of teaching, resources, time and people

4. Counselling

*   Liaison with others on a one-to-one basis to resolve sensitive problems

*   Formulating the development of self-esteem and appropriate behaviour in others

5. Personal Traits

*   Sense of order and thoroughness

*   Ability to work with others as a team

FORMAL QUALIFICATIONS

Diploma of Teaching, Capricornia Institute of Advanced Education
Resource Teachers Course Certificate
Early Literacy In-Service Tutor Training
BA Three units completed by part-time studies

OTHER FACTS ABOUT ME

Am prepared to relocate subject to career employment opportunity ... have no personal circumstances which would inhibit travel or rostered work attendance requirements ... take pride in a high standard of personal grooming and the ability to remain calm in busy situations ... am no stranger to travel or hard work ... reference letters can be provided if required

CONTACT ADDRESS: 33 Fairfield Street, Kedron 4031

Résumé of:

MARIA GIORDANO

Tel: 07 3322.9310
Email: maria@image.com.au
3/57 Bellevue Street, Ithaca 4059

OBJECTIVE

To apply my organising, data management and communications skills to appropriate tasks with public relations and/or corporate image objectives.

SUMMARY OF CREDENTIALS

- Special event organisation
- Communications with media contacts
- Production of professional membership newsletter (1,750)
- Some editing and proof-reading
- Researching and compiling specific mailing lists
- Thoroughly experienced in word processing and graphics software

SAMPLE OF CAREER ACHIEVEMENTS

- Coordinated social and business functions for dealing room staff
- Catered a buffet luncheon once a month for approximately 30 people
- Organised meetings and travel arrangements
- Liaised with media — print and radio
- Arranged a weekend conference for Hongkong Bank staff
- Produced a Monthly Economic Report which entailed:
  - meeting the deadline, i.e. ensuring media received copies before the embargo
  - liaising with printers and mailing house
  - ensuring correct distribution
  - negotiating with general public in regard to the Report and determining whether they were eligible for a copy
  - ensuring correct distribution of the Report to Hongkong Bank worldwide
  - implementing a cheaper and more efficient method of producing labels

MARIA GIORDANO   **Page 2**

EMPLOYMENT RECORD

Hongkong Bank Limited   **October 1994 - June 1997**

Personal Secretary to Chief Economist
Secretary to Chief Manager Administration
Secretary Administration Department
Receptionist

USEFUL TRAINING

Commercial Education Society
Credit Grade awards for studies and exams in Shorthand and Typing

Commercial Business College
Secretarial and Business procedures Course Completed 1993

Résumé of

HENRI KRIEL

---

86 Serpentine Crescent, Moonah 7009   (03) 6227 3045

OBJECTIVES

• To contribute to, or lead, Export Marketing Strategies and Negotiation in an industrial, commercial or service industry environment.

• To apply over 20 years' commercial experience, international trading and business skills acquired through such appointments as Production Planner through to General Manager and Member, Board of Directors to identifying sales prospects and increasing revenues though exporting. In the process have access to useful contacts developed within Europe, South-East Asia and USA to facilitate accomplishing new business development objectives as appropriate.

MAIN KNOWLEDGE AREAS

My main knowledge areas are:

• Export Sales Support

• International Trading

• Customer Liaison - Domestic and Overseas

• Sales Data Analysis

• Market Research - Domestic and Overseas

• Import and Export Practices

• Agency Management

• Warehousing and Distribution

• Forecasting and Budgeting

• Tender and Proposal Preparation

PRODUCT SPECIALITY

My commercial accomplishments have been achieved within the furniture, paper products, laminating and stationery sectors. In addition, I have a good knowledge of wines and an ability to apply my marketing skills where equipment associated with vessels and naval requirements are involved. I am no stranger to marketing to both the Public and Private sector and dealing with retail and wholesale customers.

PROFESSIONAL AFFILIATIONS

• Member, Rosny Park Businessmen's Club

• Former Charter President, Rotary Club

• Former Member of Board, National Furniture Manufacturers' Association

• Graduate, Royal Naval Academy, Dartmouth

CAREER RECORD

Furniture Manufacturers Association — past 7 years
Technical Director and Member of Board of Management

Import / Export Wine Industry — 3 years
Manager Operations

Sales Marketing — 1 year 10 months
PVC Stationery — Sales Representative

Naval Career — 12 years
Concluded commission in 1982

PERSONAL

Permanent Resident of Australia since 1982 ... prepared to relocate subject to employment opportunity ... am able to converse in Danish, Swedish, Norwegian, English and German ... Referees will be provided on request.

Career Profile of:

ANDREW YOUNG

58 Greenhill Road   Email: ayoungsales@spacenet.com.au
UNLEY SA 5061   Tel: (08) 8482.9501

CAREER OBJECTIVE:

To utilise twenty years successful and rewarding commercial experience to obtain a management position in sales or product marketing with an established company in the field of consumer products.

My career development plan is to earn appointment into an executive level marketing role or divisional general management.

CAPABILITY SUMMARY:

- DEVELOPED and implemented marketing programs for internationally known brands of high volume consumer products.

- SUPERVISED product development and improvement from conception to market release.

- PARTICIPATED in and coordinated the development of sales objectives and strategies.

- EXPERIENCED in management and direction of national advertising campaigns supported by substantial production and media budgets.

- NEGOTIATOR of major accounts with proven record of success managing sales and support personnel in their territories.

- SOUND COMMERCIAL SKILLS in accounting, budgeting, inventory control, margin retention and analysis of sales and market trends.

RELEVANT TRAINING AND EDUCATION:

- Advertising Certificate — Adelaide College of TAFE

- Commerce Certificate — Individual subjects at Adelaide College of TAFE

- Fortune Creative Selling Skills Program — Fortune Management Services

- Management Course 'Total Quality Commitment' — Quality Training Centre

Andrew Young _____ **Page 2**

PROFESSIONAL CAREER RECORD:

FAIRWEATHER LIMITED **1993-1998**
(Appliance Manufacturer)

Retrenched when the manufacturing and trading operations of Fairweather Limited ceased on 20 February 1998.

Joined as a **Senior Sales Representative** and promoted to **Product Manager — Microwave Ovens** following Fairweather's decision to manufacture microwave ovens in Australian under licence, commencing in 1997.

Broad function was to develop overall marketing programs for microwave ovens. To participate in and coordinate the formation of sales objectives and strategies, advertising and promotional campaigns and to ensure the execution of these programs.

Major Achievements:

* Increased territory turnover 270% during a three-year period by developing new and existing business.

* Rapid promotion in recognition of demonstrated ability to plan and implement wide range of advertising, promotional and marketing programs and strategies.

* Identified and persevered with the implementation of revised data-gathering procedures for quality control fault analysis which previously had failed to capture all true costs of operations.

* Developed clear market profiles for two brands of ovens and worked up new styling and promotional formats to meet those profiles.

* Produced the new product brochure in Australia as a major step to support this new profile.

ALAN J SMITH ASSOCIATES **1991-1992**

Bought into a partnership servicing the clothing industry. Major achievement was to increase receipts by 100% over a two-year period without any appreciable increase in operating costs.

Andrew Young _____ **Page 3**

PROFESSIONAL CAREER RECORD continued:

GEC Australia Ltd   **1979-1990**

Commenced as **Commerce Trainee** with Industrial Products Division, responsible to the Master of Apprentices.

Transferred to Consumer Products Division as **Assistant** to Advertising and Sales Promotion Manager, responsible for maintaining financial records of a multi-million dollar budget; supervision of work-in-progress; liaison with product managers; supervision of production of brochures, point of sale and packaged promotion material.

Appointed **Advertising and Sales Promotion Supervisor**, responsible to SA State Manager. Responsibilities included following through promotional plans with retailers; placing subsidised advertising space; organising venues for and staging of trade releases and promotions.

Later successfully performed as **Sales Representative** for three years and was promoted to **Metropolitan District Manager** for two major brands. Trained, counselled and developed metropolitan representatives to achieve sales and profit objectives.

Promoted to **Product Marketing Manager** for Room Air Conditioners, Dishwashers and Heaters. Functions included:

* Marketing Programs
* Sales Objectives and Strategies
* Advertising and Promotional Programs
* Pricing Policies
* Inventory Controls
* New Product Potential Appraisals
* Methods for Field Testing Merchandising Programs
* Analysis of Market Trends and Sales Potential

REFERENCES WILL BE PROVIDED WHEN REQUESTED

JOHN DYSON

15 Hopetoun Crescent, Croydon 3136   (03) 9485 9136 (H)

OBJECTIVE

To obtain a challenging position with particular emphasis on advertising, sales promotion and public relations in a progressive organisation which expects a high level of performance and commitment from its executives.

SUMMARY

More than fifteen years of executive level experience in advertising, sales promotion, public relations and sales management. A proven track record in achieving results through managing and advising people. Planning, organising and communicating, together with an eye for detail, and sound administrative ability are the key skills offered to an employer who needs a problem solver.

WORK EXPERIENCE

ADVERTISING: Marketing Plans; Campaign Planning; Developing and Controlling Budgets; Media Selection and Analysis; Corporate Advertising; Consumer Advertising; Industrial Advertising; TV, Radio, Press, Outdoor Advertising; Sales Literature; Catalogues; Point of Sale Material; Packaging; Direct Response Advertising; Advertising Agency Operation; Prospect Identification; Market Research; Production Techniques; Copywriting.

SALES PROMOTION: Contests; Competitions; Incentive Programs; Conferences; Sales Aids; Trade Shows; Exhibitions; Distributor Tie-In Programs; Trade Promotions; Display Techniques; Merchandising; Initiated a number of successful sales and profit generating promotions.

PUBLIC RELATIONS: Media Releases; House Magazines; Annual Reports; Conventions; Meeting Arrangements; Product Launches; Media Liaison; Sports Sponsorships; Developed several sports sponsorships into major televised events.

SALES MANAGEMENT: Contract Negotiation; Key Account Liaison; Sales Forecasting; Budgeting—Expense and Sales; Expense Control; Sales and Management Training; Customer Relations; Territory Organisation; Staff Supervision; Dealer Recruiting and Set Up; Distributor Control and Development; Distribution Networks; Financial Management; Investment Recommendations; Credit Control.

SUBSTANTIAL TRAVEL EXPERIENCE: Have organised successful seminars overseas; am familiar with Pacific and Asian areas; have made familiarisation trips to Singapore, Hong Kong, Philippines, New Zealand, Hawaii, Noumea, Fiji and Tahiti in the last three years; have lived and worked overseas and travelled extensively in USA and Europe.

CAREER PATH

1993-98   National Advertising Manager, Ampol Group of Companies in Australia
Control of all Advertising, Merchandising, Sales Promotion, Public
Relations, Corporate and Sports Sponsorships, Corporate Standards

1987-93   Merchandising and Advertising Manager, Ampol Australia Ltd
Control of Advertising, Merchandising, Sales Promotion, Publicity, Sports
Sponsorships, Sales Training

1986-87   Dealer Development Manager, Ampol Australia Ltd
Design and Implementation of effective Training Programs in Business
Administration, Sales Development, Merchandising Techniques, Sales
Promotion

1984-86	Regional Sales Manager (Vic)	Ampol Australia Ltd
1982-84	State Sales Supervisor (NSW)	Ampol Australia Ltd
1980-82	Sales Representative	Ampol Australia Ltd
1979-80	Sales Representative	Email Australia Ltd
1976-79	Promotions Assistant	Australian Trade Commission, London

BUSINESS EDUCATION AND TRAINING

- Fellow of the Advertising Institute of Australia since 1992
- Have lectured on marketing and advertising for two years to students studying for the Travel and Tourism Diploma, School of Business Studies, Mentone Technical College
- Advertising Manager's Certificate, School of Visual Arts
- Sales Management, Australian Institute of Management
- General Management Course, Sydney
- Developing Executive Potential, Australian Institute of Management
- Finance for Non-Finance Executives, Australian Institute of Management
- Running Successful Seminars, The Training Company
- Business Communications, Australian Institute of Management

OTHER FACTS

Am prepared to travel widely if appropriate, to maximise employment opportunity and career development potential. Would consider relocation if necessary.

An employer or client of my services would be assured of tasks being approached with commitment and resolution. Like to be assigned difficult tasks involving important results.

Derive personal satisfaction from seeing younger people I've trained progress in their careers. Enjoy many varied relaxation pursuits. Am involved in local soccer administration and occasional voluntary PR for local clubs.

REFERENCES WILL BE PROVIDED ON REQUEST

Professional Profile of:

ROGER LAFONTANT

Tel: 08 8847 9330

Credentials for Appointment to a Responsible Position involving The Arts and their Creative and Financial Management Direction

---

SUMMARY

Over fifteen years' creative and professionally rewarding experiences within artistic endeavours ranging from musicianship, film, TV commercials, theatre, television, lecturing, composing, scripting, voice characterisation, authorship and arts production management. Have a strong commitment to quality, innovation and effective leadership of creative people

PRECIS OF SKILLS AND EXPERIENCES

- Project management

- Production of events, shows, film media, educational courses

- Budgetary management

- Script creation and consulting

- Sourcing, evaluating and selecting artistic talent

- Direction of productions for both youth and adult audiences in film, TV and theatre

- Promotional strategies and media relations

- Management of artisans, actors, production crews, subsidiary services

- Creation of artistic concepts, production outlines, pre-production planning and costing

- Extensive knowledge and use of contractual practices and copyright (Intellectual Property) specifically for actors and writers

- Composition of scores and themes

MANAGEMENT TRAINING

Television Directors Course, (Australian Film Television and Radio School) 1996
Producers Course, plus **Production Management Course** (Australian Film and
Television School) 1995
Industrial Relations (ATUTA) 1996
Psychology of Negotiation and Conflict and **Advanced Human Behaviour** (Continuing
Education, University of Adelaide) 1997
Effective Decision Making and **Leadership Styles** (WEA) 1996

SIGNIFICANT PERSONAL DEVELOPMENT EXPERIENCES

Selection for and twelve months' study as a Student Actor at NIDA...Membership of
Management Team of a Professional Association...Actors Equity Sub-Committee
Member...Award of Jazz Piano Scholarship to study in USA for 12 months
...Participation in and active role at many conferences and seminars associated with the
Arts Industry within Australia and overseas...six semesters as a student at the
Conservatorium of Music, Sydney...Actors Training for three years at Belvoir Theatre
...Participation in radio for Print Handicapped...established and developed own small
business operations including creative talent agency

PROFESSIONAL AFFILIATIONS

Writer Full Member of Australasian Performing Right Association (APRA) ...
International Union of Puppeteers (UNIMA ... SA Puppetry Guild ... Arts Law Centre of
Australia

PERSONAL DATA

Am capable of extended hours of work...no stranger to tight deadlines and budgetary
restraints...secondary education completed at Kensington High

CONTACT ADDRESS

14/269 Stafford Street, Hackney 5069

LIST OF PRODUCTIONS, VIDEOS AND PORTFOLIO
AVAILABLE ON REQUEST

STEPHEN TUMIM

---

97 Adamson Circuit, Fairfield 3078   Telephone: (03) 9573.9247

CAREER OBJECTIVE

- To become the first officer of a modern airliner

CURRENT EMPLOYER

Southern Aviation Pty Ltd, Grade 2 Flight Instructor   Since November 1996
- Have flown predominantly throughout Victoria, with some experience in Tasmania, New South Wales and Queensland
- Selected to evaluate competitive company with a view to takeover

WORK EXPERIENCE

- Prior to aviation employment, worked as a labourer, cleaner, barman and gardener from which I saved hard to help fund my flying training program and overseas tour during which I visited several aviation centres

QUALIFICATIONS

- Current Commercial Pilots Licence — (Nationwide Aviation Space Academy, 1996)
- Current Flight Radiotelephone Operator Licence with 10 words per minute morse code endorsement
- Senior Commercial Theory subjects — (anticipate satisfactory results May 1998)
- Class 4 Instrument Rating — (NASA 1996, anticipate Class 1 by October 1998)
- Grade 2 Flight Instructor Rating — (anticipate Grade 1 by December 1998)
- 1150 hours Aeronautical experience in single and multi-engine aircraft involving charter, instruction and aerial photography
- Mathematics, Physics, Chemistry, English and Chinese studied to HSC level — (Mentone High School, 1993)

ADDITIONAL EDUCATION AND EXPERIENCE

- Tutored Year 11 Mathematics — Private Students
- Piloted groups of Scouts in company of airline pilots over eight month period during 1997
- HSC Pure Mathematics — Camberwell TAFE College, 12 weeks part-time
- Celestial Navigation course — Dept of Adult Education, 10 weeks part-time
- Experienced engine fire over Bass Strait in Piper Aztec
- Accompany Flying Doctor on days off on IFR flights throughout Victoria to experience co-pilot type environment

LEADERSHIP QUALITIES

- Initiated, organised and led groups of flying students to:
  - . Government Aircraft Factories
  - . Department of Transport Flying Unit
  - . Point Cook Aviation Medical Course
  - . Ansett Flight Training Centre
  - . Australian Airlines Maintenance Base

- Take particular pride in ensuring my students reach their goals on schedule, maintaining the highest safety standards

- Overseas travel through 10 countries including:
  - . 8 weeks' working in London
  - . 3 months' solo through Europe, UK and USA
  - . 4 weeks' study at the Language Institute, Philippines

EXCELLENT HEALTH

- Meet the requirements for the issue of an Airline Transport Licence
- Sporting interests: Swimming, lifesaving, tennis, cycling, football (including club football)

MEMBERSHIP OF RELATED ASSOCIATIONS

- General Aviation Member — Australian Federation of Air Pilots
- Branch Member — Royal Aeronautical Society
- Associate Member — Aviation Medical Society

PERSONAL DATA

- Believe my strongest assets towards my chosen career are my self-disciplined professional attitude, attention to safety and eagerness to learn more to develop the highest standards possible. Find no difficulty in accepting the authority of my seniors and particularly enjoy working in a team environment

- Keen interest in photography which has extended to developing a collection of contrasting cockpit prints

REFERENCES

- Available on request

RESUME OF

JILLIAN CARTER

54 Helen Street, Embleton, 6062
Tel: (W) 9443.1766 (H) 9484.1980

CREDENTIALS FOR REVIEW BY THE
WA SOCIETY FOR DISABLED CHILDREN FOR THE POSITION OF
SOCIAL WORKER — FREMANTLE REGION

CAREER SUMMARY

More than fifteen years' involvement in human care including extensive formal studies and practical work locally and overseas. In particular, I have been keen to develop specific capabilities in the human need areas of the disabled, the emotionally disturbed, and women's mental and physical health.

PRECIS OF COMPETENCE

*   INDIVIDUAL COUNSELLING AND CASEWORK - people with disabilities and their families, people seeking assistance with birth control and sexuality issues

*   GROUP WORK - people with disabilities, their siblings, parents and spouses

*   HEALTH EDUCATION / HEALTH PROMOTION - authored and co-authored many publications, designed programs, led seminars and held offices in many community organisations

*   THERAPEUTIC TECHNIQUES - Crisis Intervention, Bereavement, Adjustment to Disability, Personal Growth and Self-Awareness, and Family Therapy

*   COMMUNITY WORK - applied procedural techniques within organisations as well as in the field, thorough knowledge of health and welfare services

*   DESIGN OF SELF-HELP PROGRAMS - able bodied and people with disabilities

*   TEACHING - experienced in teaching within primary, secondary and tertiary education environments, as well as within public sector organisations and community education settings

*   RESEARCH - into health and welfare service facilities and their users has been extensively undertaken, also many submissions have been developed

FORMAL QUALIFICATIONS

Postgraduate:
Bachelor of Social Work, University of Western Australia, 1992
Graduate Diploma in Communications (Distinction), University of Technology, Sydney, 1990

Undergraduate:
Bachelor of Arts (Sociology), Murdoch University, 1979

PROFESSIONAL ASSOCIATIONS

Member, Australian Association of Social Workers
Member, Spinal Social Workers Group, WA
Member, Welfare Sub-Committee Paraplegic and Quadraplegic Association
Former Member (4 years), ANZ Society for Epidemiology & Research in Community Health
Member and Former State Executive Committee Member, Community Aid Abroad, WA

EMPLOYMENT RECORD

Current:
Social Worker at Prince Henry Rehabilitation Centre since August 1993

Previous:
These have included such positions as **Senior Health Education Officer**, Health Commission
of SA; **Health Promotion Coordinator**, Royal Prince Alfred Hospital; **Tutor** for WEA and
Dept of Community Health University of Adelaide, plus School of Community Medicine and
Department of Social Work, University of WA; **Clinic Coordinator** and **Director of
Counselling** at the Preterm Foundation; **Education Officer** at the Family Planning
Association and Primary and Secondary Teacher

PROFESSIONAL DEVELOPMENT

Workshops:
Family and Therapy, Death and Dying, Relationships, Communications and Counselling
Techniques, Gestalt, Counsellor Training, Self-Transformation series, Teamwork and Time
Management

Miscellaneous Student Attendances:
Medicine and Society plus Sex and Society - Dept of Sociology, University of WA; Child
Psychology - Harvard University; Teaching Methods plus History and Philosophy of
Education - Catholic Teachers College

PEOPLE WHO KNOW MY WORK WELL

Peter Jennings, Senior Educator, Prince Henry Rehabilitation Centre
(W) 9443.1761

Dr William O'Sullivan, Psychiatrist and Medical Consultant, Prince Henry Rehabilitation
Centre
(W) 9443.1768 or (AH) 9439.3819

Paula Gerald, Social Worker, Prince Henry Rehabilitation Centre
(W) 9443.1768

KEN MORTON

58 The Grand Parade   Tel: (H) 5593.4731
SURFERS PARADISE 4217   (B) 5588.3910

**Credentials for employment in any facet of Credit Control Management
and/or Sales Ledger where an employer can be assured of conscientious,
efficient service**

QUALIFIED BY:

Many rewarding years in all phases of Credit Control and Investigation.
Background includes training and practical experience in Accounting, Financial
Analysis, Law & Contracts and Staff Supervision. Am no stranger to difficult
tasks, tight schedules, responsibility and accountability.

SUMMARY OF EMPLOYMENT ATTRIBUTES:

- Have demonstrated excellent attention to detail, organisation and time
  management

- Ability to work independently, take direction from or lead others; able to fit in
  and work well with people at all levels

- Consistently met and regularly exceeded objectives and schedules in credit
  and accounting tasks

- The following areas of commercial experience have prepared me well:

Credit Management	**Administration**
Credit Policy	Sales Ledger Management
Debt Control	Accounts to Trial Balance
Cash Flow Analysis, Forecasting	Reconciliation (Manual & Computer
& Reporting	Data Files)
Trading Terms	Data Entry-EDP Facilities
Collection Practice & Procedures	Monthly Statistics
Litigation Processes	Staff Supervision & Training
Solicitors' Briefings	Manual to EDP System Conversions
Collection Agency Expense	Compiling & Maintaining Accounts/
Reduction	EDP Procedure Manuals
Supplier Contract Administration	Customer Account Queries
Credit Investigations	

ACHIEVEMENTS OF NOTE:

- Reduced debt level from 5% to 0.05% in less than 3 years in international hotel chain

- Cleared 90% of old accounts, i.e. in excess of 6 months, within the travel industry

- Implemented effective credit and trading policies and practices as my employer expanded from 6 to 22 hotel establishments

- Designed and led implementation of a debt progression policy with substantial improvement in cash flow

- Earned many commendations from my supervising managers on accuracy, timeliness and detail of credit status reports

- Acquired useful knowledge when preparing documentation for recovery of debts through litigation

- Able to maintain sound customer relationships within the administration of credit function

- Proven record of thoroughness in processing credit applications

- Know well the importance in credit control of efficiency of internal communications with the Finance, Marketing and Sales functions

RECORD OF RESPECTED EMPLOYERS:

Paradise Palms Hotel Ltd (Conference and Banqueting Complex — 550 rooms)
Position: Credit Controller/Sales Ledger Supervisor (5 1/2 years)

Credit Management Agency
Position: Special assignments in credit management consulting
                for Hilton International Hotels (7 months)

Milton Travel
Position: Credit Controller (2 years)

Ramada Hotels
Position: Special Investigation Assignments

PERSONAL DATA:

- Sound working knowledge of commercial law relating to credit and contracts
- Believe that, though my special expertise is credit administration within the Hotel, Tourist and Travel industries, my skills and knowledge are readily transferable to other areas of commerce
- Member, Institute of Credit Management

KEVIN J SEARLE

49 Howard Street   Tel: (H) 3830.3005
BEENLEIGH 4207   (B) 3970.3977

OBJECTIVE:

I am keen to apply my skills in information systems, systems reform and sound commercial acumen to the creation of genuine benefit to clients in consultancy tasks. My technical management background and demonstrable skills in managing professional staff, together with tenacity in complex problem solving, support this objective.

I enjoy not only the investigative aspects but also the creation of imaginative solutions integrated with advanced data processing and telecommunications technology. As an experienced executive with substantial cost centre responsibilities, I am able to contribute to overall organisational analysis and re-structuring, if warranted, in a variety of environments.

CAREER SUMMARY:

Twenty years' practical experience in data processing and information management, with a thorough grounding in the earlier period in programming and systems analysis and design. My most recent professional contribution has been within a highly competitive commercial environment where exceptional results have been achieved. As a member of the executive management team employing 600 staff, we have produced the highest productivity per sales dollar on record and in two years increased revenue from $60 million to $200 million within the industry sectors of Government, Education, Medical, Commercial and Finance. This involvement in an information technology, marketing and customer support organisation has usefully built on my prior role in planning and implementing information management systems for a multi-faceted marketing oriented manufacturer over a seven and a half year period.

ACHIEVEMENT SUMMARY:

- **Information Strategy**

Moving computing into the hands of the users for planning, operational word processing applications.
Established new framework for information systems by top-down planning:
  . Identification of key result areas and key tasks required for the company to achieve its objectives of the five year plan.
  . Creation of a data model reflecting the total company-wide view of data.

- **Planning & Development**

Directed the development of manpower plans to support Information Service functions for the South Pacific Region for many sites. Identified Key Result Areas and Tasks required for business objective achievement. Developed information strategies to support these. Created data model for total business logistics information.

- **Planning & Development continued**

Computer Operations: Directed development of computing and communications for South Pacific Region which incorporated connection to world-wide network. Improved scheduling and reliability performance of data centres through new procedures and standards development.

Office Automation and Administration: Developed plans for automating large-scale office communications. Installed 52 integrated workstations and led telecommunications requirements analyses study for an interstate network. Directed review of functional areas resulting in organisational and procedure reform which included development of National Procedures documentation.

- **Staff Management**

Recruited, trained and directed work of 30 staff and contractors. Focused on morale and productivity improvement successfully.

- **Commercial Development**

Researched, evaluated and recommended restructuring of purchasing, warehousing and distribution functions. Guided subsequent change process.

EMPLOYMENT RECORD:

Information Services Manager, South Pacific Region
CONCEPTS CORP   July 1992 to present

Business Systems Manager
RECKITT & COLEMAN   Oct 1984 to June 1992

Systems Analyst
CUSTOM CREDIT   Dec 1980 to March 1984

Systems Analyst/Programmer
STERLING PHARMACEUTICALS   May 1980 to Dec 1980

PROFESSIONAL DEVELOPMENT:

- Management Development Program
  Australian Administrative Staff College, Mount Eliza - 1991

- Systems Analysis - Advanced Techniques
  National Computing Centre, United Kingdom - 1981

JOHN RADOVAN

51 Mulwalla Crescent, Turramurra 2074
Tel: (02) 9498 9301 (home)

CAREER OBJECTIVE

My objectives are to broaden my experience and skills in computing, particularly in communications, local area networks, and in computer languages in an employment environment which would make use of my investigation, diagnostic, analytical and system solution skills.

CAREER SUMMARY

Formally trained in electronics, telecommunications, data transfer systems with progress into data processing, particularly data capture, technical specifications, programming, computer interfaces and system testing.

EMPLOYMENT FOCUS

Would prefer an employer engaged in service to clients in computing, software and/or telecommunications.

COMPUTING SKILLS

- Specification and design of computer systems from user's requirements
- Problem analysis and design of system solution
- Programming substantial technical systems (Language: primarily BASIC)
- Design of communication protocols
- Interfacing of different computers for the transfer of information
- Hardware testing and diagnostic procedures
- Interfacing of external hardware to computers
- Barcoding
- Use of Digital Command Language (RSX 11M+), Personal Computer DOS, CPM
- Use of DOS and Windows packages (Lotus, Word, Open Access, etc.)
- Technical drawing

EDUCATION

Bachelor of Engineering, University of New South Wales, graduated 1979
Specialised in Electrical Engineering (Communications and Electronics)

PROFESSIONAL DEVELOPMENT

Technical
Electrical Wiring, Sydney College of TAFE
Microprocessor System Development, University of Technology, Sydney
Measurement and Instrumentation, University of New England

Management/Communications
Management Training, In-Company
Communications, In-Company
Technical Writing and Communication, Sydney College of TAFE

CAREER RECORD

Landsdowne Limited   **January 1992 - 1998**
Information Systems Officer

Responsibilities: Specification, design and implementation of automatic data capture
system (data transfer directly from scientific instruments to computer). Evaluation of
commercial software and hardware. Cost/benefit evaluation. Programming for workstation
computers.

Landsdowne Limited (Refinery)   **January 1989 - December 1991**
Instrument/Energy Engineer

Responsibilities: Installed and upgraded computing system associated with energy
metering. Also supervision of instrument workshop. Specification, design and
commissioning of instrumentation systems. Analysis of energy consumption for energy
reduction.

Landsdowne Limited (Mill)   **June 1988 - December 1988**
Shift Chemist

Responsibilities: Supervision of factory process workers and overall control of factory
process.

Landsdowne Limited (Central Laboratory)   **1982 - May 1988**
Instrument Officer

Responsibilities: Maintenance of laboratory instruments, design and manufacture of
factory instruments, testing and evaluation of commercial instruments, troubleshooting
technical equipment. Fulfilled technical study and advisory services on overseas
assignments to Europe, USA and Fiji.

Résumé of

VERNON BORG

41 Errington Way, Crows Nest 2065   Tel: (02) 9436.3912
_____

OBJECTIVE

To obtain a supervisory position in Manufacturing with a medium-sized company. I have special expertise in packaging products, but would consider alternative production environments.

SUMMARY OF EXPERIENCE

Many years' rewarding experience in the Packaging Manufacturing industry covering supervision, planning, recruiting, technical services, purchasing, estimating, quality control, warehousing, accounting and administration.

EMPLOYMENT RECORD

PEP PACKAGING PTY LTD   1984 - 1998
Production Manager   **10 years**
Reporting to the Group Manufacturing Director. Responsible for the efficient production of the Flexible Packaging Division by means of production planning, maintenance programs, quality control and labour controls. There were 90 personnel employed in this Division, consisting of skilled, semi-skilled and unskilled.
Key Achievements
- Instigated a production planning system to achieve a better work flow
- Increased efficiency by means of better methods and reduction of staff, together with effective waste, maintenance and quality controls
- Arranged new plant layout to achieve a better flow of work and control
- Organised staff training and safety programs
- Established a canteen and suitable amenities for the employees
- Arranged for EDP labour and material controls to be instigated

Warehouse and Distribution Manager   **2 years**
Reporting to the Managing Director. Responsible for the efficient receiving, storage and distribution of manufactured and merchandise products.
Key Achievements
- Reorganisation and layout of warehouse to achieve extra storage area and a better flow of work
- Installation of stock control, which in turn enabled a reduction in stock holdings

Costing Officer   **2 years**
Reporting to the Group Manufacturing Accountant. Responsible for estimating all company products and setting suggested selling prices. Also assisted in the installation of the direct costing system onto computer.

EMPLOYMENT RECORD continued

J EDWARDS PTY LTD   **14 years**
Factory Superintendent   **4 years**
Reporting to the General Manager. Responsible for the efficient running of production, storage and warehousing. Factory personnel employed - 80
Key Achievements
- Cost reductions by improved methods
- Relocation of plant and equipment to obtain efficiency by means of better work flow

Production Supervisor   **6 years**
Reporting to the Factory Superintendent. Responsible for the efficient production of the Hessian and Multiwall Division. Factory personnel employed - 50
Key Achievement
- Installation and proving of the Multiwall plant

Branch Accountant   **4 years**
Reporting to the General Manager. Responsible for the office management, estimating and accounting up to trial balance stage
Key Achievement
- Installation of costing system

SUMMARY OF TRAINING

- Productivity Course - Adelaide 1989
- In-house training in Safety, Employee and Industrial Relations
- Accountancy Certificate - North Sydney College of TAFE - part-time

COMMUNITY ACTIVITIES

- Past President of South Beach Life Saving Club
- Past Treasurer and Property Manager, South Torrens Junior Football Club
- Have served on several sporting club committees

REFERENCES AVAILABLE ON REQUEST

LAWRENCE MAJID

43 Swift Street   Tel: (W) 9283.1933
Jolimont 6014   (H) 9328.1394

EMPLOYMENT OBJECTIVE

To be employed in problem-solving tasks associated with Marketing Services, Inventory Management, Purchasing or Distribution

EXAMPLES OF SKILLS

- Stock Control and Inventory Management
- Systems Design and Reform
- Distribution Management
- Materials Handling
- Manual or EDP-Assisted Inventories (Design and/or Management)
- Purchasing Procedures
- Product Promotional Planning
- Valuable experience in distribution and supply problem-solving, particularly in scheduling tasks for the best results
- Reformed a very inadequate replacement parts shortfall system by a comprehensive program converting most of the manual systems to a computer-based system
- Associated with EDP-oriented data systems over the past 15 years and know the value of efficient outputs to stock control and problem identification

RECORD OF EMPLOYMENT

VALIANT OFFICE GROUP LTD   **February 1990 to December 1997**
(Office Furniture Specialists)

Appointed **Product Manager** and later **Product Planning Manager** at the time the Company acquired its own manufacturing premises. My initial task was the assembly and issue of the first ever catalogue of the full range of CASA products. Have also functioned as purchasing, costing, delivery coordination officer, dealt with Customs, devised EDP codes and maintained a computer-based inventory system.

My reporting relationship was to the General Manager, but for financial information accountabilities to the Group Accountant.

RECORD OF EMPLOYMENT continued

CONCORD MITSUBISHI   **1989 to 1990**
(Car Dealership)

As **Spare Parts Manager**, planned, designed and implemented total system for
stock storage and retrieval, and built computer-assisted control procedures. This
responsibility covered many varied and complex tasks in the process of fitting-out,
furnishings, design and purchase, recruiting and training staff, forms design,
briefing of and liaison with computer consultants, managing data input to new
EDP system to accommodate an inventory of 2,500 line items.

KING MOTORS LTD   **1981 to 1989**
(Car, Truck & Tractor Manufacture and Assembly)

Initially appointed Dealer Credit Controller, subsequently promoted to Assistant to
Market Research Manager and later to Pre-Production Stock Controller and
Replacement Parts Computer Programs Coordinator.

HMV (ENGLAND) LTD   **October 1977 to September 1980**
(Record Manufacture, Marketing & Promotion)

From early responsibilities in despatch and warehousing later assumed
accountabilities for distribution management, total inventory management and
contributed to marketing and A and R management. Copyright research and
liaison featured during this period, as well as the development of relations with
publishers, distributors and the media.

REFERENCES AVAILABLE ON REQUEST

RESUME OF

GRANT PRATT

49 Fairweather Drive
Seven Hills 2147   Telephone: (H) 9729 3917

**CREDENTIALS DEVELOPED DURING THOROUGH TRAINING AND
PRACTICAL EXPERIENCE FOR EMPLOYMENT IN DESIGN, DETAIL AND/OR
DRAFTING IN MECHANICAL OR ELECTRICAL FIELDS**

OBJECTIVE

To undertake job tasks and assignments for an employer where thoroughness and hard
work would be appreciated and appropriately rewarded. To increase my knowledge in
mechanical engineering, design and development of new products and build on my
recent training in CAD.

CAPABILITY SUMMARY

- Mechanical Design & Drafting
- Machine Drafting & Detailing
- Electrical Design Drafting
- Hydraulics & Pneumatics Systems
- Electro-Mechanical Engineering
- Pressure Vessels (Design & Detail)
  - Water Chillers

- Sheet Metal Drafting
- Production Layouts
- Engineering Drafting & Detailing
- Programming PLC
- Design of Plastic &
  Aluminium Packaging

EDUCATION ACHIEVEMENTS

- Completed CAD Drafting course at Parramatta TAFE College, 1997

- Industrial Fluid Power, Controls and Hydraulics, plus Refrigeration and Air
  Conditioning. Additional part-time studies at TAFE Colleges, 1993-94

- Mechanical Engineering Certificate (Granville TAFE College) 1987. Chose electives in
  Industrial Fluid Power and Engineering Computations (EDP/Graphics)

- Architectural Drafting Certificate. Completed 3 stages successfully of 4 stage course,
  1983

- Public Speaking (In-company Training Course)

GRANT PRATT   **Page 2**

EMPLOYMENT RECORD

GEC AUTOMATION & CONTROL PTY LTD   **October 1995 to July 1997**
Engaged as a contractor as an Assistant Engineer/Design Draftsman involved with the day to day problems of engineering the traffic control lanterns. Design modifications to existing products, plus development of prototypes.

CABLEMAKERS AUSTRALIA   **February 1991 to September 1995**
(Electronic and Communication Equipment)
Employed as a Design Draftsman, I was involved in the drawing and creation of a plastic box to hold electronic components and meter for measuring electricity usage.

BORG-WARNER   **1987 to 1991**
(Air Conditioning/Water Chiller Production)
As Detail Draftsman in the Drawing Office was assigned to new product development (turbo packs), electrical control panels and air-cooled condensers (sheet metal work). Liaison with production.

UNICORN GROUP (AUSTRALIA) PTY LTD   **1983 to 1987**
(Hardware Manufacturers)
Earned promotion quickly from Process Worker to Tool Setter to Supervision. Operated and repaired many types of machines (e.g. drilling, auto-sawing, riveting, thermo-plastic and specialised sharpening). Contributed to many improvements through time and motion analyses, production quality and significant reduction in reject rates.

TONY ARCHER & HENRY COLE   **1979 to 1982**
(Architects)
Drawing Office. Started out as print boy and office boy. Later promoted to Draftsman assigned to alterations of plans for office buildings and Department of Education schools.

PEOPLE WHO KNOW ME WELL

Mr P Nicholls   Mr T Howard
Senior Design Engineer   Chief Engineer
Cablemakers Australia   (Former Manager)
Tel: (B) 9690 3188   Borg-Warner
                                           Tel: (B) 9606 3111

COMPREHENSIVE WRITTEN REFERENCES AVAILABLE ON REQUEST

Capability Statement

TIMOTHY O'SULLIVAN BEng (Mech)

PERSONAL

Nationality:	Australian	Address:	Kenworth Associates
Education:	BEng (Mech), Sydney		PO Box 392, Stepney 5072
Availability:	1 month domestic	Email:	timprojects@ozemail.com.au
	2 months overseas	Phone:	(08) 8949 3139

SCOPE OF PROJECT / TASK EXPERIENCE

Project Initiation
Detailed planning...economics...development strategies...costing...scheduling ...budgeting...interface with authorities and clients...work studies...environmental impact statements

Project Management
Group coordination all disciplines...site organisation...staffing...site administration and cost control...quality assurance...material procurement...configuration management... occupational health and safety...scheduling...employee relations

Project Commissioning
Facility commissioning schedules...plant and equipment logistic support systems ...setting to work, whole of life maintenance and spares support

PROJECT PRECIS

Establishment of an oil company	New Guinea
Pipeline construction and operation	South Australia/NSW
Ethanol plant development	NSW
Logistic support oil search	Australia & New Guinea
Commercial buildings, bulk storage, warehousing, material handling	Australia wide
Industrial gas turbine application development/scope	USA & Australia
Ship's bridge simulator	RAN, Australia
Logistics support systems—new vessel construction	RAN, Australia
Revamp metal products manufacturing facilities	New Zealand
New plant and equipment—concrete, quarrying, sand extraction	Victoria

Value of projects directly managed exceeds $1.5 billion present value terms

TYPE OF INDUSTRY	**POSITIONS HELD IN INDUSTRY**
Manufacturing	Manager...Consultant
Service Organisations	Manager...Contract assignments
Oil and Gas	Engineer...Operations Manager...Assistant General Manager...Consultant
Dept of Defence Support Industries	Consultant...Project Manager

BRIEF OUTLINE

PETROLEUM AND NATURAL GAS EXPERIENCE

PETROLEUM

- Seaboard and inland terminal development, construction, operation
- Consolidation of inland distribution facilities
- Road and rail distribution; plant and equipment
- Environmental studies
- Employee relations, award negotiations
- Product quality control
- Aviation fuelling facilities, design, construction, operation
- Tankship agency, coastal tankship operation
- Mainframe and PC networking

Establishment of oil distribution and marketing facilities New Guinea

---

NATURAL GAS TASK EXPERIENCE

Pipeline
- Route selection
- Land acquisition
- Design
- Contract development
- Construction and commissioning

Pipeline operation
- Manning
- Training
- Operational plant and equipment — procedures
- Gas turbine compressor station development

CNG
- Facility development shore based — shipboard for a CNG fuelled vessel

---

OVERSEAS ASSIGNMENTS

USA, Singapore, UK and New Guinea

Résumé of:

ED FERRIS
38 Swift Street, Albury 2640
Tel: (B) 02 6027 4933 (H) 02 6031 3974

OBJECTIVE

To be assigned Project Management responsibilities with a major construction company where my extensive practical experience, training and technical knowledge can be applied.

SKILLS AND EXPERIENCE SUMMARY

- Cost management up to maximum turnover of $2m per month
- Supervision of direct labour earthworks and machinery
- Control of sub-contractors
- Internal cost management—manual and computer
- Procurement and evaluation of quotations
- Contractor—client relations
- Road and pavement design
- Ordering and stock control of all materials
- Preparation, supervision and adjustment of mix designs
- Quality control of concrete batched and placed
- Control of all testing for acceptance of concrete
- Design and supervision of joint layouts
- Preparation and valuation of claims
- Fast track building construction
- EXCEL spreadsheets to advanced level
- Checking formwork designs

PROFESSIONAL EMPLOYMENT RECORD

THIESS CONSTRUCTIONS   March 1995 to date

Project Engineer, Wodonga and Coolac Contracts - Arbitration
Provide technical assistance and advice to Barrister and Solicitors for the arbitration hearing.

Concrete Engineer, Darling Harbour Project
Programming and supervision of all concrete placement and repairs. Supervision and scheduling of reinforcing, steel placement. Checking and modifying formwork systems. Design of concrete pumplines for high level pours. Redesign and modification of reinforcement and structural steel arrangements.

Project Engineer, Hume Highway & Federal Highway - Bicentennial Road Projects
Engineer responsible for all aspects of concrete road construction. Also included was supervision, cost and monitoring of drainage works, road pavement and traffic diversion. The design and modification of all concrete mixes as required The design of 8 x 100 km/hr traffic diversions. Design of additional drainage structures and culverts.

ED FERRIS   **Page 2**

PROFESSIONAL EMPLOYMENT RECORD continued

THIESS CONSTRUCTIONS continued

Site Engineer, Federal Highway Duplication - ACT
Supervision, programming and monitoring of earthworks, hydraulics, traffic management and road pavement construction. The design of all blasting of 60,000 cub m of rock within 50 m of houses and large reservoir. Planning and implementation of traffic management scheme, including temporary traffic lights and several traffic switches.

Plant Manager, Hamilton, Victoria
Supervision, design and quality control of concrete production from a medium-sized concrete plant.

WORKING EXPERIENCE PRIOR TO GRADUATION

- Engineering Trainee with both Department of Main Roads and the Water Board for six months. Organised men and materials for construction work (structural concrete and roads)

- Casual Bar Attendant and HSC tutor (Maths) during my four years of study

- Two years' useful clerical and administrative experience within the Water Resources Commission

TERTIARY EDUCATION ACHIEVEMENTS

Bachelor of Engineering : Major: Structure. University of New South Wales.
    Graduated 1993
    Achieved 13 Credits and no subject failures
    Thesis: Wind Effects on Tall Structures
    Major Projects: Hydraulics and Concrete Hinges

PERSONAL

Prepared to relocate...used to travelling and site assignments throughout New South Wales...enjoy good health...recently completed speed reading training for personal development...plan part-time studies in Business Management to commence shortly...Member of the Institution of Engineers of Australia (MIE Aust).

Résumé of:

JULIA ARMSTRONG

85 Warrington Crescent, Wangara 6065
Telephone: (08) 9382 9563

CREDENTIALS FOR AN APPOINTMENT WITHIN
THE COMMUNITY HEALTH SERVICE PROFESSION

OBJECTIVE

I am keen to implement my long-term ambition to be engaged in the provision of community health services in a rural environment. My pursuit of relevant qualifications, research into the nature of this work, and appreciation of living in non-metropolitan areas all support this career objective.

QUALIFICATIONS

- Registered Nurse following training at Royal Perth Hospital, completed 1993

- Completed studies for Family Planning Certificate in 1994

- Completed studies successfully for Midwifery and graduated in March 1997, now a registered Midwife

SPECIAL PERSONAL DEVELOPMENT EXPERIENCES

- Completed Communications and Self-Assertion program conducted by Marriage and Family Guidance Council of WA. In addition, as part of staff development, I participated in a course concerning reflective listening and counselling techniques

- Gained much from 11 months in the Intensive and Coronary Care Unit at Royal Perth Hospital in 1994/95, including being a member of cardiac arrest team

- Completed diverse assignments in home care and relief nursing, geriatric care for an agency over three months

- Observed procedures and administration of two Baby Health Centres in Metropolitan Perth, plus Child Abuse Prevention program and sub-normal children school visits

- Learnt a considerable amount through assignments at Prince Henry Hospital involving treatment for gestational diabetes, hypertensive disease of pregnancy, complicated deliveries, neo-natal intensive care, and artificial insemination and IVF procedures

- A 12 month period travelling within Europe, Thailand and Africa increased my interpersonal skills, appreciation of diverse cultures, and the ability to handle contingency situations

- Received an early initiation in office administration and procedures through casual employment experiences during student period as Accounts Payable Clerk, Filing Clerk and as Receptionist within commercial firms

EMPLOYMENT RECORD

Prince Henry Hospital (Midwifery Training)	March 1996 to October 1997
Princess Alexandria Hospital	October 1995 to February 1996
Perth-Wide Nursing Agency	August 1995 to October 1995
Royal Perth Hospital	June 1994 to May 1995 and June 1990 to June 1993

PERSONAL

I enjoy excellent health, maintain my own fitness program, and have a determination to achieve good results in human care while applying high professional standards. My interest in rural areas has developed through an association with the Margaret River Region over several years, my active involvement in bushwalking and a general appreciation of community life in non-urban environments. I am aware that I have much more to learn and plan to complete the Associate Diploma Community Health Nursing by correspondence, as well as the Mothercraft Certificate.

I am no stranger to driving in remote areas and capable of basic vehicle maintenance and emergency repairs.

Referees will be provided on request

Résumé of:

William REGALE
8/37 Prince Henry Street, Carlton 3053
email: regale@bigpond.com.au
(03) 9889 3711 (W) or (03) 9743 3130

CAREER OBJECTIVE

To work in a client support role where my skills in information systems, data processing and librarianship can be utilised in resolving information management problems through data processing.

SUMMARY OF SKILLS

*   **Computing**

As manager of one of the largest Australian corporate library's computer systems for the last 6 years, I have gained experience in:
* PC systems, particularly communications and word processing packages
* the VAX VMS operating system and DCL programming
* programming in the INFO language

As part of my studies in the Graduate Diploma in Business (Data Processing) at Victoria University of Technology, I have gained experience in:
* programming in Cobol, Pascal and Prolog
* relational database systems
* system analysis and design
* data communications and communications networks

*   **Management**

As manager of this corporate library with a staff of six and an annual budget of $600,000, I have gained experience in:
* budgeting and the strategic planning of resources and service needs
* management of staff including their performance appraisal and personal development
* written communications including many user manuals and guides
* marketing a service function to 35 operating units and subsidiary companies
* time management

*   **Experienced Librarian**

As a librarian for over 14 years, in both private and public sectors, I have gained considerable experience in:
* design and management of computerised information retrieval systems including reference databases and videotex
* library management and associated systems

William Regale   **Page 2**

TERTIARY QUALIFICATIONS

* Completed to date two-thirds of Graduate Diploma in Business (Data Processing) at Victoria University of Technology

* Graduate Diploma in Information Services, Royal Melbourne Institute of Technology, 1983

PROFESSIONAL DEVELOPMENT

* Management Development Program, In-house

* Performance Appraisal and Personal Development Review, In-house

* Interpersonal Communications Program, In-house

CAREER EXPERIENCE

1996 to November 1997   Manager, NAB Infoservices, Corporate HQ

1991 to 1995   Senior Information Officer, NAB

1990   Travelling Overseas

1985 to 1989   Senior Information Scientist, MIM

1984 to 1985   Librarian, State Office Block Library

PROFESSIONAL ACTIVITIES

* Member of the Library Association of Australia. Have held several executive positions in interest groups of the Association since 1988

* Member, Institute of Information Scientists (UK)

REFERENCES WILL BE PROVIDED ON REQUEST

Résumé of:

PAULA VISHINSKY

83 The Avenue, Rosewater 5013
Tel: (h) 08 8654 9327 (w) 08 8330 1888

Credentials for Employment Tasks Involving Marketing, Marketing Services and Promotional Strategies

---

OBJECTIVE

To apply my skills and knowledge in Marketing, Sales and Administration to an employer conscious of projecting a positive image in the quest for sales growth. Consumer products sector is my primary goal with a preference for fashion products.

PRECIS OF CURRENT COMPETENCIES

Sales	Stock Control
Distribution	Brand Development
Sourcing Products	Merchandise Ranging
Buying	Supplier Negotiations

EXAMPLES OF MY PROFESSIONAL DEVELOPMENT

- As Product Manager, carried out total responsibility for image and sales of a prestige label and supervised the support roles of accounts, warehouse and administration

- Organised product catalogues including the management of photographers, graphic artists, printer

- Developed point-of-sale merchandise (concepts, design, production)

- Forecasting, budget preparation and control analyses

- Setting up stock control systems for high profile watches, accessories

- Setting prices for wholesale purposes

- Organising of showrooms

- Making sales presentations

- Visits to liaise with and supervise certain operations in Hong Kong company

PAULA VISHINSKY   **Page 2**

CAREER RECORD

W K Phillips & Co - Wholesaler/Retailer - 19 months

Harris Media - Advertising Agency - 14 months

Olivetti Aust Pty Ltd - Office Technology

Concurrent with studies was employed for several years in part-time duties mainly in the Retail Industry involving sales, merchandising and stock management of accessories and fashion products

SKILLS DEVELOPMENT TRAINING

Marketing Certificate - Part-time studies with two years' satisfactory progress to date at TAFE College

Adelaide Business College (Word Processing, Fax, Telex, Dictation, Grooming)

HSC Matriculation, Rosewater High School

OTHERS FACTS ABOUT ME

No impediments to travel or relocation interstate or overseas subject to career opportunity ... thrive on difficult tasks and the pursuit of challenging and reasonable goals

REFEREES WILL BE PROVIDED ON REQUEST

ALISON CROMPTON

60 Wunda Street, Lilydale 3140
Tel: 9368.9413 (H) or 9728.9504 (leave message)

CAREER OBJECTIVE

An opportunity to work within the Communications or Public Relations area is my goal. I seek employment in an organisation where high personal standards, efficiency and integrity are expected and rewarded. Am prepared to work shift-work where necessary. Available for employment immediately.

KEY AREAS OF KNOWLEDGE AND SKILL

Media Relations

- Wrote, distributed and followed up media releases

- Wrote scripts for and recorded several community service announcements

- Arranged and participated in many interviews—television, radio and print

- Negotiated involvement of local media with special event being organised

- Organised for media celebrities to attend special events and participate in community service announcements

- Directed celebrities in their roles on day of special event

- Arranged and supervised photo sessions, plus distribution of photos to the media

Special Events/Organisational Skills

- Negotiated sponsorship of events with local businesses and corporations

- Initiated seven country fund-raising events including major projects in Newcastle and Wollongong

- Researched feasibility of conducting events in different areas

- Monitored progress of events through planning stages, involving liaison with police, councils, community service groups, volunteers, sponsors and media

- Directed entire operations on day of special event

ALISON CROMPTON   Page 2

KEY AREAS OF KNOWLEDGE AND SKILL continued

Special Events/Organisational Skills continued

- Designed artwork for leaflets, sponsor and entry forms and liaised with printer to finished art stage

- Responsible for financial success of programs

Public Relations

- Lectured community groups on the role of the Heart Foundation

- Represented Heart Foundation on many occasions at charity dinners, fairs and other public events

- Handled wide variety of enquiries from general public, government and other organisations

QUALIFICATIONS

Certificate of Public Relations, Sydney College of TAFE, 1996-97. Two years' part-time study. Completed subjects: PR Practice, Art Direction and Print, Business Communications (Publicity to be completed in Melbourne in 1998)

Certificate of Business Studies (Travel and Tourism), North Sydney College of TAFE, 1994-95. One year full-time, plus part-time study. 12 units completed with mostly 'A' levels

EMPLOYMENT RECORD

Heart Foundation   **Mar 1996 to Mar 1998**
Field Projects Officer

Queensland Tourism Commission   **Jan 1995 to Mar 1996**
Travel Consultant

Entertainment Centre   **Nov 1993 to Feb 1994**
Ticketing Outlet Supervisor

Sandhurst Town (Tourist Attraction)   **Apr 1993 to Oct 1993**
Tour Guide

REFERENCES WILL BE PROVIDED AT INTERVIEW

To: **MR P KENDRICK**
         General Manager, Human Resources
         Urban Transit Authority

Career Credentials for Appointment as:

MANAGER, OCCUPATIONAL HEALTH & SAFETY SECTION
POSITION NO: 902458
URBAN TRANSIT AUTHORITY

From: **MAXWELL SOUTH**
         State Rail Authority
         Tel: (w) (08) 9283 1934 (h) (08) 9808 1932
         46 Bathurst Street
         LEEDERVILLE WA 6007

CAREER OVERVIEW

WA State Rail Authority   **1977 - Present**

Occupational Hygienist	(2 yrs 9 mths)
Industrial Chemist	(11 yrs 9 mths)
Cadet Chemist	(5 yrs 11 mths)

RECENT PROFESSIONAL HIGHLIGHTS

Achievements in the last 21/2 years:

- Established an Occupational Hygiene Advisory Service in WA State Rail

- Introduced and implemented a management system for control of chemicals at the workplace including material safety data systems, inventories, labelling and training for employees

- Successfully provided senior management with advice and strategies for resolution of critical industrial disputes relating to Occupational Health and Safety (OH & S)

- Assisted in the establishment of OH & S on a project management basis including preparation of budgetary proposals

- Managed the activities of external OH & S consultants on critical projects including development of codes of practice and handling synthetic mineral films and development of chemical control strategies

- Prepared and submitted successful proposals to senior management for purchase of occupational hygiene testing equipment

- Assisted in the introduction of training programs for OH & S Workplace Committees

PRECIS OF CREDENTIALS FOR VACANCY

Management of Staff:

- Acquired thorough knowledge of EEO Policies and Procedures at WA State Rail

- Planned, directed and controlled the OH & S and compensation activities for up to 150 subordinates

Health & Safety:

- Held organisational wide responsibility for OH & S Policy for WA State Rail over extended period

- Developed many strategies for identifying, assessing and controlling harmful toxic materials and physical agents in the workplace

PRECIS OF CREDENTIALS FOR VACANCY continued

Workers Compensation and Rehabilitation:

- Carried out investigation and reported to Executive Management on:
  a) Workers Compensation instances throughout the organisation
  b) implications of legislative changes

Specialist Advice to Management:

- Provided a consultancy service to line managers personally and through subordinates

- Researched, analysed data, developed recommendations and reported to Executive Management on very sensitive matters including, for example, productivity of 'selected duties' employees

- Devised many computerised methods for statistical control and early identification of OH & S problem areas requiring attention and corrective action

- Provided advice and strategies for resolution of sensitive industrial issues and disputes

RELEVANT QUALIFICATIONS & PROFESSIONAL DEVELOPMENT

BSc (Applied Chemistry) Graduated from University of Western Australia 1982 achieving Credit or higher awards in sixteen subjects

Participated in several courses in managerial subjects, for example Job Selection, Safety Awareness for Supervisors, Occupational Health for Industry, Positive Power and Influence, EEO awareness; Five specialist courses in computing and 15 in Industrial and Scientific subject areas

PROFESSIONAL PARTICIPATION

Committee Member, Standards Association of Australia; Member, Australian Institute of Occupational Hygienists; Member, Health & Safety Panel - Australian Welding Association; Member, Australian Corrosion Association; plus credentials as authorised signatory for many categories, National Association of Testing Authorities; Chairman, Government Agencies Chemicals Management Group. Participant in Annual Conferences Australian Institute of Occupational Hygienists 1994 - 1997

REFERENCES WILL BE PROVIDED ON REQUEST

RESUME OF:

CATHY MATTHEWS

Unit 3, 86 Sutherland Road, St Albans 3021   Tel: (03) 9384.9265

CAREER OBJECTIVE:	To be appointed a Flight Attendant/Cabin Crew Member with an Airline.
PERSONAL PRESENTATION:	Trained as a Fashion and Photographic Model at June Dally Watkins and subsequently pursued that career for three years in Sydney and Melbourne.
PHYSICAL FITNESS:	Am a regular tennis player and participate in aerobic classes three times per week. Enjoy excellent health and maintain an active schedule of physical fitness, e.g. daily swimming.
ADMINISTRATIVE SKILLS:	Trained as Secretary at Metropolitan Business College for six months and subsequently have been employed in secretarial and administrative responsibilities for a total of four years.
OVERSEAS TRAVEL:	Spent 12 months in Israel studying Hebrew on a Kibbutz, 1993. Have toured Hong Kong, England, Denmark, Italy, Austria, United States and South Pacific in recent years.
CUSTOMER SERVICE:	Have worked in Retail Sales within the Fashion industry. Know the value of patience, cash-handling efficiency and good humour in customer relations.
MEDICAL TRAINING:	Completed successfully Red Cross First Aid Certificate program (ten weeks - 1998).
FORMAL EDUCATION:	Completed Year 11 and further studies at Richmond College of TAFE
PERSONAL:	Date of Birth: 3 June 1971 I maintain high standards of personal grooming and my sense of humour in tense situations. I am no stranger to hard work, long hours and enjoy meeting people.

Professional Profile of:

MIKE OVENS

57 Hindmarsh Terrace, North Adelaide   (08) 8423.9416

EMPLOYMENT OBJECTIVE

To obtain appointment as a senior Human Resources/Personnel professional, reporting to the General Manager, with responsibility for a broad range of personnel activities.

CAREER HIGHLIGHTS

. Appointment as Chief Manager, Personnel for Avalon Oil and Gas, prior to sale to Esso Exploration and Production Australia

. Established and managed comprehensive personnel function for Avalon O&G reporting to Managing Director

. Recruited 25 overseas oil and gas technical specialist staff for Avalon O&G

. Project Manager for retrenchment program involving over 200 people in Avalon O&G, following oil price collapse

. Established and managed personnel function for Avalon Australia Ltd, Corporate Headquarters staff

. Member of In-Company Working Party (4 people) set up to coordinate major involvement in an Inquiry by the Industries Assistance Commission (IAC)

. Secretary of several UK companies following acquisition and involved in change of domicile of these companies from the UK to Australia

MAIN CAPABILITY AREAS

. Human Resource Management	. Retrenchment/Redeployment
. Recruitment of Senior Professional Staff (Overseas and Local)	. Marketing of Personnel Services
. Strategic Planning/Manpower Planning	. Job Measurement
. Organisation Development	. Communication
. Succession Planning/Career Review	. Budgeting/Control
. Remuneration Management	. Administration
. Counselling	

PROFESSIONAL EXPERIENCE

AVALON OIL AND GAS   **1995 — 1998**
Manager, Personnel and Administration
Manager of a team of nine professional staff and two support staff responsible for all facets of personnel management for approximately 500 staff, 200 contractors and 100 wages employees, including:

.   remuneration and benefits   .   industrial relations
.   workers compensation   .   training and development
.   occupational health and safety

Key Achievements
.   Recruited key professional staff
.   Developed personnel policies and practices
.   Managed personnel aspects of rapid growth in organisation (increase of 440 employees over 1994-1996)
.   Developed charter, strategic plans, budget ($2.5m) for Personnel Department
.   Managed personnel aspects of rapid downturn in organisation
.   Developed guidelines for managers on the selection of people for retrenchment — in conjunction with Office of Commissioner for Equal Opportunity (SA)
.   Management responsibility for health and safety program (described by SA Minister of Labour as 'a model for all other firms')
.   Major role in setting up Queensland office and relocating 25 staff
.   Role of catalyst in major organisation changes
.   Introduced computerised personnel management information system (CHRIS)
.   Management responsibility for comprehensive training and development program
.   Developed progressive Affirmative Action plan

AVALON AUSTRALIA LIMITED
Manager Personnel, Group Personnel   **1991 — 1995**
Manager of a team of seven people responsible for a broad range of personnel services for staff in Avalon Australia Headquarters (about 400 staff) including subsidiaries. Advised corporate general managers and functional managers on personnel policy and issues. Responsible for cadetship and scholarship schemes, liaison with secondary and tertiary education institutions.

Key Achievements
.   Established an effective team and service, held in high repute by senior managers
.   Recruitment of professional staff during a period of growth
.   Company-wide 'job-posting' system introduced
.   Introduction of career reviews for corporate headquarters staff
.   Developed policies for and administered retrenchment scheme
.   Participant in Avalon senior personnel managers' policy development meetings
.   Introduced new arrangements for Avalon cadets and scholarship holders and for housing Avalon students

PROFESSIONAL EXPERIENCE continued

Senior Administration Officer,
Marketing Administration Policy   **1988 — 1989**

Responsible for administrative aspects of Avalon's role as contractor and marketing agent, including preparation of papers for annual meetings with the Board.

Regular contact with Chairman and Board Members.

PROFESSIONAL EDUCATION AND DEVELOPMENT

1996   Invited participant to workshop organised by Australian Mineral Foundation in association with Australian Petroleum Exploration Association

1995   Bachelor of Legal Studies - University of New South Wales

Strategic Personnel Management - Australian Graduate School of Management

Industrial Advocacy and Negotiation - In-Company

1993   Advanced Management Program - Australian Institute of Management, Victoria

1991   Communication in Management - Charles Sturt University, Mitchell Campus

1978   Bachelor of Arts - Macquarie University

PROFESSIONAL MEMBERSHIPS / ACTIVITIES

- Member, Australian Human Resources Institute (MAHRI)

- Executive Member, NSW Workshop in Innovation & Entrepreneurship 1992-93

- Guest lecturer on aspects of personnel management at AHRI (SA), University of South Australia (MBA students in organisational change)

JENNY DUNCAN

---

51 President Avenue, Curtin 2605   Tel: (02) 6285 3975

CAREER OBJECTIVE

An Administration, Coordination, Budget Control, Secretarial role for a busy executive who needs skilful help or as office supervisor/manager for administrative support functions in a challenging, busy task-oriented organisation.

KEY ASSETS OF ABILITY AND EXPERIENCE

Budgeting and Management: With partner established new operation devoted to personal development and encouragement for each of its members. Administered complex budget totalling $185,000 over period of time. Jointly planned and achieved growth of investments and property holdings.

Purchasing: Made majority of purchasing decisions to ensure maximum results from available funds. Managed continuous stock inventory, negotiated with suppliers and maintained high credit rating by prompt attention to accounts. Reviewed results with partner on a quarterly basis and decided on new acquisitions.

Motivation and Development of Others: Worked hard to help group members achieve their potential. Regularly engaged in personal counselling and arranged programs to stimulate new endeavours. As new members joined, following close consultation with partner, plans were made for the development and accomplishment of group goals.

Travel and Transportation Management: Decided on changing transport requirements as group size grew, assisting in evaluation and selection of new equipment, both motor transport and marine. Managed maximum utilisation of vehicles to meet often conflicting demands and changed schedules. Coordinated and supervised three relocations of group's premises and re-established facilities and local community relations.

Other Duties requiring Supervisory Skills: Proposal preparation, nutrition, taxes, building and grounds maintenance, social activities including VIP functions, catering, training and contributing to community service groups.

SPECIFIC ACHIEVEMENTS

In partnership with my husband, this experience was gained through 21 years loyal attention to our family. Two sons at University and one teenage daughter currently studying for HSC are the favourable balance sheet results. A successful husband and a high equity in home and two investment projects are also proud results.

PERSONAL DATA

This combination of family and community service involvement has prepared me well for handling crises and organising matters. Reduced need for these skills at home encourages me to apply them in a business environment.

ROSA van RIJN

10 Firth Street   Telephone: (02) 9748.1392 (H)
CARRS PARK 2148   or leave message on (02) 9906.3122

OBJECTIVE

Human Resource Development

To apply my practical experience of and qualifications in training, development and recruitment to challenging opportunities in Human Resource Development either in a Training or Recruitment role.

CAREER SUMMARY

Employment in both public and private sector working with a variety of people in a range of professional, technical and administrative jobs. Proven track record in the field of Personnel, in particular Training and Recruitment, has given me a solid base from which to work on topics ranging from Interviewing through to Induction, Problem Solving, Management Development, Management of Change, Customer Service. Organisational change challenges rather than deters me.

PROFESSIONAL DEVELOPMENT AND FORMAL TRAINING

- Completed a degree part-time and achieved Bachelor of Arts in Business Studies, 1992

- Registered as Trainer with Local Government Training Board and gained Associate member status with the Australian Institute of Training & Development, 1988

- Career Development Workshop, 1997

- Communication and Negotiation, 1996

- Management of Change, 1995

- Counselling Skills and Career Counselling, 1995

- Management Development Training, 1988

- New Approaches to Identification of Training Needs, 1987

- Diagnostic Skills Course, 1987

- Selection Interviewing, 1985

PROFESSIONAL CAREER RECORD

OCCIDENTAL Life   **June 1997 - March 1998**
Staff Development Officer

Major Responsibilities
*   Developing, organising and conducting the following training courses:
    *   EEO Awareness Program
    *   Team Leader Development Program
    *   Induction
    *   Interview Skills
    *   Assertiveness Training
    *   Developing Personal Growth Plans
*   Providing consultancy and facilitation skills to teams, groups, departments in the following areas:
    *   Problem Solving
    *   Team Building
    *   Business Planning
    *   Process Observation
*   Providing full range of recruitment from the drawing up of advertisements through to interviewing for staff in office services, cashiers and accounts areas
*   Involved in a wide variety of personnel matters, including:
    *   TTD Claims
    *   Unpaid Leave
    *   Rehabilitation of Staff
    *   Regrading
    *   Statistics

Key Achievements
*   Successfully developed and ran two Interview Skills courses to enable supervisors to become fully involved in interviewing. The objective was achieved and to quote the manager, "Their confidence and ability to conduct an interview was increased dramatically. Thank you for a 'spot on' course."

*   Developed new training exercises for use in the Management Development Program which encompassed building trust, leadership, team building, communications, providing feedback, utilising the experience and relating it to the work situation.

*   Prepared a paper on ideas for marketing EEO awareness sessions to managers.

ROSA van RIJN   **Page 3**

PROFESSIONAL CAREER RECORD continued

SOUTH SYDNEY CITY Council   **Sept 1986 - March 1997**
Department Personnel Services

Assistant Personnel Officer (1 year)
Personnel Officer (5 years)
Senior Personnel Officer (4 years 5 months)

Major Responsibilities

- As Assistant Personnel Officer involved in the recruitment and selection of junior and professional staff across an organisation of over 6,000 staff. Included drawing up advertisements, interviewing, organising selection tests, drawing up letters of appointment, putting together the internal vacancies bulletin, giving advice on recruitment matters to departments.

- As Personnel Officer, assisted in the provision of training and meeting the training needs of staff across the organisation. Developed and ran a range of courses - Induction, Skills, Health and Safety, Industrial Relations. Assisted in the development and running of the Council's Clerical Trainee Scheme. Pioneered first line management training.

- Following my promotion to Senior Personnel Officer, similar duties were involved with regard to skills training, a major role in the development and running of a Management Development Program for middle and senior managers.

Key Achievements

- Developed and conducted successful Management Development Program for 70 senior and middle managers which allowed me to develop a program to meet individual needs

- One of a team of three trainers involved in taking a large department through a management of change operation, including a week's residential for the top 30 managers, a range of sessions to help the change process and evaluating the whole program one year later

- Pioneered the use of computer-based training packages in the Council. Designed training packages in the areas of Selection Interviewing and Equal Opportunities

- Jointly responsible for the success of the Council's Clerical Trainee Scheme (24 trainees) through supervision, feedback, counselling and a commitment to its success

- Designed a package of information on careers and opportunities with the Council for career conventions, talks and seminars

- Conducted first Induction course after two days in the Training Section 'experience by being thrown in the deep end' - which turned out to be successful and well received

BONITA ROSSI

CREDENTIALS FOR EMPLOYMENT AS TOURISM AREA MANAGER

AREAS OF COMPETENCY

MARKETING
- Proposal Research and Preparation
- New Business Development
- Profitability of Current Business
- Hospitality Procedures
- Maintenance of Existing Accounts
- Seminar and Trade Show Organisation and Presentation
- Convention Planning

MANAGEMENT
- Budgeting and Forecasting
- Administration of Offices
- Crisis Management
- Selection and Recruitment of Staff
- Staff Counselling and Training
- Salary Administration

SUMMARY

My travel and tourism career has spanned many target groups from the general public through to Public and Private sector business travel. My work activities over the past three years have involved, for example, negotiation with Chief Executives and Managing Directors of many large companies. I have proved myself to be a valuable employee who has been promoted on merit and worked in three different positions with the same employer. I have worked hard to develop a reputation of creating innovative systems which minimise workload and maximise efficiency levels.

EXAMPLES OF ACHIEVEMENTS

MARKETING
- Won corporate business in past two months to the value of A$1.3 million
- As an experienced marketer, realise quality and efficiency have to follow client brief
- Proven ability to increase sales and concurrently maintain service levels
- Maintain a high level of service to corporate customers with no loss of business due to lack of service or skills
- Devised new strategies for obtaining corporate business
- Promoted Jetset Tours' own wholesale products to travel agents in Vic, Qld and NSW
- Researched and analysed new business development possibilities
- Recently secured two major corporate customers
- Planning and budgeting skills during management of A$16.5 million Sales Centre in Jetset Tours' Travel Centre, based in Melbourne
- Earned personal nomination for Entrepreneur Award 1996 and my team's nomination for Winners' Award and Business Travel Award 1996

EXAMPLES OF ACHIEVEMENTS continued

OFFICE MANAGEMENT
- Have recruited and inducted over 20 staff over past two years, in consulting, accounting, financial, secretarial and reception positions
- Motivated 24 subordinate staff during my management of Jetset Tours' largest Business Travel Centre in Australia
- Evaluated staff's behaviour and work efficiency — performance appraisals
- Reduced costs in the area of time usage and effective management of resources — both human and facilities
- Trained many junior staff on-the-job, alongside some formal training provided by principals

TOURISM/INTERNATIONAL TRAVEL
- Led group tours to unusual parts of the world, e.g. China, Egypt, Jordan, Israel and Russia
- Designed new document for use by sales people in business travel for clients' use when travelling
- Able to identify priorities when handling urgent travel arrangements
- Presented new products to staff with strong emphasis on the features and benefits of selling the proposed airfare, hotel or tour
- Developed new systems for the operation of the Business Travel Centre

RECORD OF EMPLOYMENT

Jetset Tours   **Sep 1994 to present**
Sales Manager VIC for Business Travel
Manager, Business Travel
Sales Executive

Australian Airlines   **Feb 1993 to Sep 1994**
Passenger Sales Agent

Great Ways Travel   **Apr 1987 to Jan 1993**
(World wide travel specialists)
Travel Consultant in London, UK

PROFESSIONAL DEVELOPMENT AND TRAINING

Manager Awareness Course, TIAS   The Management Workshop
Effective Debt Collecting, Dun & Bradstreet   TIAS Conversion Course
AFTA Fares and Ticketing II   QANTAS Travel Agents' Course
QANTAM Course, Fares, Ticketing, etc.   Business College, TAFE College

OTHER FACTS ABOUT ME

No personal restrictions on relocation...no attitudes which would deter me from striving to accomplish difficult tasks well...no stranger to interpersonal effectiveness with diverse ethnic groups...no restrictions on passport for overseas travel...enjoy excellent health and healthy range of leisure and education interests...experienced training in Time and Stress Management...some knowledge of French...countries visited include:

United Kingdom	Scandinavia	Europe
United States	Russia	Turkey
Israel	Jordan	Egypt
South America	South Africa	Kenya
Mauritius	India	Thailand
Malaysia	Singapore	China
Tahiti	Fiji	

CONTACT DATA

Address: 327 Cheltenham Road, Cheltenham 3192
Telephone: (03) 9501.3795 (H)
Email: brossi@gateway.net.au

Professional Profile of:

PAT JACKSON

3/193 Toorak Road, Toorak 3142
Telephone: (03) 9832.7317

OBJECTIVE

To apply eighteen years' experience in development, construction and project management as a senior member of a management team in full-time employment. I am no stranger to managing many projects simultaneously, tight schedules, high-level negotiations, solving complex problems and appraising both new project feasibility and design.

MAIN CAPABILITIES

- Development Project Management
- Contract Negotiation & Administration
- Sub-Contractor Management
- Property Acquisition & Sales
- Relationships with Government & Local Council Authorities
- Site Inspections

- Property Management
- Financial Analysis
- Tender Specifications
- Design Aptitude
- New Buildings & Renovations - Domestic, Commercial & Industrial
- Consultant Appointment & Liaison

PROFESSIONAL EMPLOYMENT

Structural Ways Pty Ltd   **February 1988 to current**

A partnership wherein I have been engaged in a wide variety of construction projects including, for example, quality new houses, residential developments, renovations and commercial buildings in the Melbourne Metropolitan area. Activities carried out:

- Property acquisition and/or sales
- Negotiation of contracts
- Legal contracts
- Marketing self and product
- Costs recording

- Feasibility studies
- Bank negotiation
- Estimating
- Budgeting cash flow

- Virtually all manual and trade activities associated with building
- Professional and client negotiations and contracts
- Architectural and Local Authority negotiations, re: design elements
- Hire and supervision of labour and sub-contractors
- Establishing and maintaining accounting procedures, debt collection

Mainstream Investments   **November 1984 to January 1988**
Development Manager

Responsible for several major projects concurrently at various stages of development with
cost/profit centre accountability. Also, joint venture relationships and thorough reporting
systems were elements of assigned duties, as well as feasibility studies, Board-level
representations, selection of architects, finance sourcing, and legal and contractual
relationships. Sub-contractor evaluation and selection featured across all trades and
services and liaison with relevant authorities was a key requirement. Reorganising and
financing sales or lease back arrangements whether with partners or purchasers were
further responsibilities.

Previous Employment

Prior employment included tasks associated with accounting and finance, production
operations, O & M, marketing, organisation development and systems design with a
number of major public companies.

FORMAL QUALIFICATIONS

*   Bachelor of Commerce, Melbourne University

PERSONAL DATA

My preference is for a Melbourne-based position, though I am willing to travel
extensively subject to nature of career opportunity.

Able to commence appropriate employment within three weeks of acceptance.

REFEREES WILL BE PROVIDED AT INTERVIEW

DENNIS POLLA

34 Rawson Parade, Scarborough 4020
Tel: (07) 3523.8117 (H)

CREDENTIALS FOR A POSITION WITHIN THE RETAIL INDUSTRY

CAREER OBJECTIVE

Group Management and/or Merchandise Buying responsibilities within the Head
Office of a Retail Organisation

CAREER SUMMARY

My sales, buying and management career has spanned over 13 years in specialist
retail sales operations and front-line customer service. I have the motivation, drive
and determination to achieve results and a genuine commitment to customer
satisfaction - generating significant levels of profit for my employer.

AREAS OF COMPETENCE

- Merchandise Buying and Product Ranging
- Wholesale and Manufacturer Negotiations
- Advertising and Sales Promotion
- Sales Negotiation and Public Relations
- Sales Budgeting, Reporting and Analysis
- Product and Market Place Analysis
- Store Planning and Layouts
- New Store Openings
- Inventory Control
- Franchise Management
- Warehousing - Receiving and Dispatch
- Staff Motivation, Supervision, Training and Development
- Operations and Administration

MEMBERSHIP

Member - Retail Management Institute of Australia

DENNIS POLLA   **Page 2**

PROFESSIONAL BACKGROUND

1) ORGANISED special and volume buys - captured and advanced market share

2) LIAISED with manufacturers and suppliers to ensure competitiveness in the marketplace, and prompt delivery and service schedules

3) ESTABLISHED realistic levels of stock holding - attained desired stock turnover in line with set budgets

4) ACHIEVED and EXCEEDED sales, gross and net profits of the areas under my control

5) SUCCESSFULLY maintained key accounts - investigated and generated new business

6) DIRECTED high standards of after-sales service, complaint handling and problem solving - received numerous customer testimonials

7) CONCEPTUALISED and ORGANISED advertising and sales promotions - stock support, display and point of sale material

8) RENDERED feedback on market trends, requirements and ideas for new product development to manufacturers

9) SOUND knowledge of franchise store operations

10) OPENED new stores and DESIGNED innovative store and department layouts

11) ENSURED high standards of merchandise presentation, continually aiming to improve the sales per sq m of the departments

12) TRAINED, SUPERVISED and MOTIVATED staff in policy procedures, selling and work practice skills

RECORD OF RESPECTED EMPLOYERS

K-Mart Home Improvements   **1994 - Present**
Sales Management

Mad Barrys Home Improvements   **1989 - 1993**
Department Sales Manager

Norman Ross Stores Limited   **1983 - 1987**
Sales Consultant - Then promoted to Assistant Store Manager and finally to Store Manager/Group Relieving Manager

OTHER FACTS

I am capable of representing my company in all situations and am able to work independently or as part of a team. I enjoy new and challenging opportunities, am success oriented and continually aim to meet high standards of time management, priorities and interpersonal skills.

Professional Profile of:

SAM WHEAT

PO Box 381
Thornlie 6108   Telephone: (08) 9212.4381 (H)

CREDENTIALS FOR A RESPONSIBLE POSITION IN THE TOURISM / TRAVEL INDUSTRIES

OBJECTIVE

To further my career interest in tasks related to Travel and Tourism as past experiences in the hospitality and aviation/tourism industries have been particularly fulfilling and informative.

Self-organisation, communications, time-critical schedules and administrative procedures are aspects of worklife to which I am no stranger. My personality is soundly based on interests in assisting others. In such tasks I derive significant personal satisfaction.

AREAS OF COMPETENCY RELEVANT TO CAREER OBJECTIVE

Travel Management
- Qantam System Manual
- Reservation Procedures (Land, Air and Sea)
- Ticketing
- Customer Service
- Agents Relationships
- VDU Operating & Word Processing
- Hospitality Procedures

Supervisory
- Staff Management
- Self-Organisation and Time Management
- Administration
- Cash Management
- Crisis Management
- Small Group Function Organisation
- Good Team Member

SPECIAL QUALIFICATIONS

- Australian Airlines In-Company Programs:
  i) Advanced Passenger Contact
  ii) Austair communication and reservation procedures
- Travel Agent's Course, International Training Centre
- WA Hotel, Motel Training Centre Course
- Qualified in First Aid, Red Cross (current)
- Wine and Cheese Graduate, College of TAFE
- Registered Swimming Instructor, WA Amateur Swimming Association

SOUND TERTIARY EDUCATION

- Diploma of Social Sciences, Curtin University of Technology. Majored in Communication, Psychology and Sociology

- Bachelor Degree, Majoring in Administration, part-time student in concluding year

- Primary Teacher's Certificate, University of South Australia

EMPLOYMENT RECORD

Communication	Teacher - WA Dept of Education	3 years
	Teacher - SA Dept of Education	12 years
Aviation	Australian Airlines of Australia	2 1/2 years
Hospitality	Matilda Bay Hotel, Fremantle	6 months
	Functions Assistant on part-time basis	
	(Board Meetings, Dinner Parties, Weddings)	
Commerce	Amway Distributor	5 1/2 years
	(Part-time business)	

PERSONAL

Most enjoy myself when very busy, yet cope with stress well by keen interests in bushwalking, electronics, photography and swimming. Am an active member of the Australian Conservation Foundation and World Wide Fund for Nature (Australia). Keen user of my own IBM PC.

An employer who expects and rewards good results brings out my best efforts to resolve business problems and find inventive solutions.

REFEREES WILL BE PROVIDED ON REQUEST

Résumé of:

MARVIN LIEBMAN

3/35 Dunblane Street, Wembley 6014
Tel: 08 9224 9358

Credentials for Employment where
thorough experience in Transport, Operations Management,
Materials Handling and Distribution is required

CAREER SUMMARY

Over nine years' employment experiences in the retail sector including increasing responsibilities in materials handling, warehousing and staff supervision. Essentially, I am practically inclined and enjoy employment tasks which demand coping with diverse problems and a busy environment. I am no stranger to directing the work of others and liaising with external sub-contractors and customers. I have succeeded well at increasing dispatch rates and reducing stock levels, containing disputes and implementing improved work practice systems.

PRECIS OF SKILLS

Storage Systems	Warehouse Administration
Purchasing	Union Relations
Transportation	Merchandising
Inventory Management	Supplier Negotiation
Staff Management	Wharf Operations
Heavy Duty Equipment Direction	

EMPLOYMENT RECORD

Tender Meats Pty Ltd   **1993 to October 1997**
Wharf Superintendent - Warehouse Foreman - Warehouse and Packing Materials Foreman

Corgi Foods   **1990 to 1993**
General Foreman - Packaging and Raw Materials

Grace Brothers   **1988 to 1990**
Assistant Manager - Retail Store

Employment prior to 1988 included the Steelworks in Port Kembla, Public Sector and the hospitality industry in a variety of positions.

PROFESSIONAL STUDIES

Completed two years' part-time study in the Personnel Administration Certificate at TAFE College, two years' full-time undergraduate studies at Curtin University and several in-company training courses such as team-building and supervisory development.

Résumé

Roger Nadler, A.V.L.E. (Econ.)

84 Wunda Street
Manly 2095

Tel: 9971 4392 (Home)
9014 9224 (Voicemail)

CAREER OBJECTIVE

To continue to progress in the real estate profession as a valuer and apply my knowledge and experience to valuation practice with an employer with high standards.

MAIN KNOWLEDGE AREAS

- Statutory Valuation Work
- Property Management
- Strata Management and Legislation
- Property Marketing
- Office Management

- Community Title Management
- General Book Keeping
- Trust Accounting
- Market Research

QUALIFICATIONS

- Associate Member of the Australian Institute of Valuers & Land Economists Inc. A.V.L.E. (Econ.)
- Registered Real Estate Valuer
- Licensed Real Estate Agent
- Licensed Strata Manager
- Licensed Business Agent

PROFESSIONAL EMPLOYMENT

L.J. HOOKER   **August 1993 — March 1998**
Property Manager
Skills Applied: Leasing Residential and Commercial Premises
                                           Property Inspections
                                           Negotiating Leases and Rent Reviews
                                           Repairs and Maintenance
                                           Arrears Control

GERRARDS PTY LTD   **July 1989 — July 1993**
Strata Manager
Skills Applied: Conducting Meetings
                                           Strata Orders
                                           Property Correspondence
                                           Building Services Administration
                                           Repairs and Maintenance
                                           Conflict Resolution
                                           Consulting Engineers Report

CAMERO REALTY   **October 1988 — March 1989**
Commercial / Industrial Leasing Manager
Skills Applied: Listing Properties
                                  Negotiating Leases
                                  Commercial Leasing Agency Agreements
                                  Lodging Development Applications with Local Government

JOHN WALKER REAL ESTATE   **July 1988 — September 1988**
Residential Salesman
Skills Applied: Listing and Selling Property
                                  Conducting Auction Campaigns
                                  Advertising Campaigns

1984 — 1988
Effectively performed the duties of Strata and Property Manager in the Real Estate
Profession

PERSONAL QUALITIES

I am a person who pays keen attention to detail, is assiduous and keen to advance in my
chosen career in the valuation profession.

5 Your Job Application Letter

Many people have difficulty writing letters. Consequently, the words and expressions used in letters are frequently awkward and poorly organised. The job seeker who writes clear, coherent and concise letters will have an advantage over others competing for the attention of an employer.

Preparing Your Letter

When you apply for an advertised position, you need to be aware that perhaps 70 others will be applying as well. Often the first applications to be rejected are the untidy ones. The rest are usually read through quickly, with the reader picking out those that are the most interesting. Your aim is to be among those that the employer decides to re-read with closer attention.

A short letter is more effective than a long letter, but more difficult to compose. The tone of writing and selection of words should convey enthusiasm and confidence.

By preparing your letter carefully, you improve your chances of gaining an interview, even if you do not have the ideal qualifications or past employment record.

Objectives

A job application letter needs to gain the reader's attention from the beginning. It should:
- state clearly why you should be considered;
- give information to back this up;
- ask for a response.

You have designed your résumé so that a copy of the same original can be sent with minor adjustments with all your job application letters. Each letter, however, must be written specifically for each job application or purpose in the job hunt.

It's not easy to write to a stranger—and it's even harder when you're writing to that person in order to apply for a job. In your letter you are trying to persuade the reader to consider you ahead of many other applicants. Your aim is to make that person interested enough to read your letter and résumé thoroughly and convince them to contact you for an interview.

Your job application letter is a good opportunity to present yourself to a prospective employer in the way you want to be perceived. It is a very different situation from when you are being interviewed—then you will have to answer the questions put to you by the employer. In your job application letter you can emphasise more easily your strongest claims for consideration. So make the most of this chance to create a good first impression.

> ☞ *Remember to highlight in your letter one key point which you feel is the best reason for you to be considered for the job.*

You can find clues to important points for your covering letter in most job advertisements. Don't be put off if you think you cannot meet all the requirements in the advertisement. If you write a good résumé and job application letter, you may still win an interview. Instead of apologising for the qualities or qualifications you don't have, emphasise those you do.

Practise in Advance of Need

It's better to draft a letter as soon as you decide to start your job hunt even though you may not have a specific employer in mind. It takes time, thought and experimentation to produce an effective one. You will need to follow up emerging opportunities promptly during your job hunt period. If you have a basic draft ready to amend, you will be better off than if you have to create one in a hurry.

Information Employers Like to Receive

The key to obtaining job interviews is to write only about things that are likely to interest the employer. Employers receive many job application letters that are like life stories—full of too much unnecessary information.

Before you draft your letter, read what employers would like to be told in job application letters, but rarely are:

- Why you decided to write to them.
- Your knowledge of any of the organisation's products, services and/or customers or clients.
- A clear statement of the type of employment arrangement you want, e.g. casual, part-time, temporary, work experience, subcontract, job-sharing, vacation or permanent full-time employment.
- Time and dates you are available for an interview.
- How they can contact you quickly by telephone, fax or email.
- The address to which a written reply should be sent.

- How to spell your name. Your signature does not always make this clear, so don't rely on it alone.

Guidelines for Your Job Application Letters

- Be specific about why you are writing.
- Don't use lined paper.
- Do not repeat the content of your résumé.
- Demonstrate that you have done some research.
- Convey enthusiasm and commitment.
- Review your past references and performance appraisals for sentences that describe you favourably.
- Balance a business-like impression with your personal style.
- Be appropriate with choice of words, but seek also to be different.
- Be brief and focus on the purpose of the letter, i.e. to gain an interview.
- Humour has no place in your letter, nor do statements of how long you have been job hunting, nor your views on the state of the world, morality, nor your personal philosophy of life.

Addressing the Letter

Address your letter by name to the person who usually receives job applications in the organisation to which you are applying. This is easy if a name has been given in the advertisement or a careers' directory. If not, make a telephone call to the receptionist or telephone operator of the organisation, state that you are a job applicant and find out the relevant name and job title. Make sure you obtain the correct spelling of the person's name.

People in the working world are usually conscious of their titles and take more notice of correspondence that is addressed to them personally. You may have noticed this with the mail you receive at home: letters addressed to 'The Occupant' or 'The Householder' are likely to be thrown away unopened; whereas that happens less frequently with those that are personally addressed.

The First Section

The first sentence of your letter is the most important. Spend some time working out what you want to say and how best to say it. You can begin the letter in a number of different ways. Most people seem to mention how they found out about the job. You could be different here.

A good way to gain the reader's attention is to start with a positive statement mentioning the qualities you have that show you are suited to being employed by this employer. Some different approaches are listed on the next page. Choose one and amend it to suit the job for which you are applying:

"A position in your firm is my goal. My enclosed résumé shows my preparation for achieving it."

"'Committed' and 'thorough' are words my past employer used to describe me. I would bring these to the job role of ..."

"I have read in the newspapers this week about your activities. Your firm interests me as one in which hard work and good customer service will be rewarded."

"Eight years of software development experience and my project planning skills prompt me to apply for your vacancy as ..."

In this first section be sure to state the type of job role you are seeking.

The Middle Section

In the middle section, provide information about yourself to show why you should be considered. Not many readers will believe you are right for the job just because you say you have the necessary attributes. The best way to interest the employer in you is to mention the contribution you feel you can make.

Choose one or two important points from your background and give enough details about them to influence the reader that you are an applicant who should be looked at more closely. Also, state that you have enclosed your résumé.

The Final Section

At the end of your letter, state what you would like the recipient to do. Is it to invite you for an interview? Do you want to know if the organisation is interested in you? Would you like your letter to be filed in case a suitable job role comes up in the future?

The final section is the right place to ask for the action you want. You may tell the reader that you will telephone at a certain time on a given date. Dates and times when you would be able to attend an interview can be included here.

As most employers are very busy, they will appreciate being able to contact you easily. They may prefer to telephone, fax or email you, rather than prepare and post a typed reply. Also, if a vacancy has to be filled quickly, it is often those applicants who are easy to contact who are invited for an interview, so include how you can be contacted.

If you do not have a telephone and/or fax, ask a friend or relative whether you may use theirs and request them to take messages for you and pass them on promptly.

A Note on Length

Although an application letter has three sections, it may be typed in four, five or six paragraphs. If you exceed six paragraphs, it is likely you are saying too much and may lose the interest of the reader. Remember, your job application letter is to raise interest in learning more about what you offer, not convey all about who you are.

Make sure your letter is neither too long nor too short. If your letter is too long, the reader may feel irritated by details that are not related to the job. The employer will not be interested in your hobbies or even your ambitions, if they have nothing to do with the job for which you are applying. The letter is about you—but only those qualities of yours that show your suitability for their employ. If you write too much about yourself, you will sound self-centred.

On the other hand, if your letter is too short, it may seem as if you do not really care about getting employed or about what sort of job you do get.

The covering letter is not the place to include the many questions you may have about the job and employer. It is best to leave your questions until the interview.

Pay and Employment Conditions

If you write about pay or employment benefits in your covering letter, you may be risking your chances of an interview. Also, if your letter requests too low a figure, you may start at a lower salary than you deserve. Worse, if you state too high a figure, you may be ruled out altogether. It is best not to mention how much you expect to be paid—leave it until the interview.

It can annoy employers if, in your letter, you ask for details of pay, deductions, hours of work, holidays and other leave, parking facilities, superannuation or flexitime arrangements.

Your letter should be concerned with your target job role and the opportunities available for you to do what you can for the employer.

Unsolicited Application Letters

Many job vacancies are never advertised, but are filled by people who have previously written to employers or employment agencies seeking work. Advertisements cost money. For this reason, many employers and recruitment consultants keep 'applicant banks'—files of people who, on their own initiative, have applied to them. Such applications are referred to as 'unsolicited', i.e. not asked for. When an employee resigns, retires, is transferred or promoted, the employer may look through their applicant bank and contact some of the people who have written recently looking for employment.

Most employers and recruitment consultants like to receive these applications. It saves them time and advertising costs when a vacancy occurs. Sending unsolicited applications has two main advantages:

- It can increase the number of your employment opportunities.
- It reduces the likelihood of competing with large numbers of other applicants.

Recruitment Brochures

Many employers put out brochures that describe their organisations. Some of these are recruitment brochures designed to interest people in joining their staff. Such publications can give you points to use in your job application letters.

Recruitment brochures describe the type of work available, the products and services provided by the organisation and possible career directions within the organisation. They usually also give some details of the experience and qualifications needed for different roles in the organisation and describe the training which may be provided after hiring.

By reading such brochures thoroughly, you may find a way in which your past can be of use to the company. This can then be highlighted in your letter.

If a brochure is not available, you might find a clue as to what to highlight through reading the employer's recruitment advertisements or checking whether they have an internet website.

Checklists and Advice for Your Letter

The checklists and advice on the following pages will help you construct a personal letter of the highest standard—one that will certainly increase your chances of obtaining that important interview.

Step-by-Step Approach

1. Complete Checklist 1 on page 165.
2. Review all the sample letters in this Guide on pages 171-177, whatever their purpose.
3. Underline phrases which appeal to you.
4. Write first draft of your letter.
5. Take a break.
6. Complete Checklist 2 (page 165).
7. Go back to the letter and rewrite it until you are satisfied that it is the best you can do.
8. Complete Checklist 3 (page 167).
9. Complete Checklist 4 (page 168).

The sample letters from page 171 onwards will give you many ideas of what to include in your letter.

Checklist 1 (Before you write your first draft)

✓

Yes No

- Have you researched your prospective employer thoroughly? ❏ ❏
- Have you amended your résumé to suit their nature? ❏ ❏
- Have you noted how to spell the employer's name and postal address correctly? ❏ ❏

Checklist 2 (Complete after you have written your first draft)

✓

Yes No

- Have you included the title of the intended recipient? ❏ ❏
- Is your opening paragraph no more than five lines? ❏ ❏
- Have you clearly stated the type of employment you are seeking? ❏ ❏
- Have you avoided using 'I' more than three times? ❏ ❏
- Have you avoided writing anything which is incorrect? ❏ ❏
- Have you avoided writing about your non-work interests, unless what you have learned from them is relevant to the job you are seeking? ❏ ❏
- Have you avoided mentioning what you expect to be paid? ❏ ❏
- Have you mentioned an achievement of which you are quite proud relevant to their services or products? ❏ ❏
- Have you indicated that your résumé is enclosed? ❏ ❏
- Have you recorded some evidence of your research into the prospective employer? ❏ ❏
- Have you avoided mentioning personal problems? ❏ ❏
- Have you asked for action in the last paragraph? ❏ ❏
- Have you mentioned when you are available for an interview and how you can be contacted? ❏ ❏

Write another draft based on what you have learned from completing Checklist 2. If all your answers have been 'Yes', check your expression and spelling after reading the following advice, then move on to Checklist 3.

Check Your Expression

It is an unfortunate fact that mistakes in a job application letter can stand out alarmingly, often causing the reader to ignore the good parts.

Now that your letter is in draft form, examine carefully the words you have used. If you do not feel confident about some of your expressions, ask a teacher, lecturer or counsellor to suggest improvements.

The following list of poorly expressed phrases have been taken from actual job application letters. Unfortunately, they would have contributed to the applicants' not obtaining interviews.

"...I hope that you will act favourably on my application. I shall await your reply with eager anticipation..."

"...You would no doubt want to employ a candidate like me next year..."

"...It must be noted that I will not be available for employment for several months..."

"...I would find it a great honour to work with you..."

"...I may not have much experience, but..."

"...I have had numerous jobs..."

"...I am desirous of employment..."

"...Please humbly accept my application..."

"...I trust you will avail yourself of my services and assuring you of my closest attention..."

"...I offer myself for your consideration..."

"...I will furnish more information..."

"...It has come to my attention that you are looking for candidates..."

"...Kindly accept the undersigned..."

These awkward phrases do not help, but make it difficult for employers to understand what you want to communicate.

Check Your Spelling

academic	excellent	pursue
achievement	experience	pursuing
ambition	extensive	recommended
application	extracurricular	referred
appreciate	innovative	semester
assistance	interview	sincerely
benefited	occurred	substantial
budgeted	opportunity	successfully
career	permanent	summarise
commitment	personnel	targeted
committed	preference	tertiary
deferred	preferred	trial
emphasis	principal (= main)	written
enrol	profession	
enrolled	proficient	

Keep a good dictionary, such as *The Macquarie Dictionary*, handy.

Checklist 3

	Yes	No
• Does the tone of your letter indicate self-confidence and respect without bragging or being too humble?	❑	❑
• Have you been careful to avoid stating only what you want?	❑	❑
• Have you avoided apologising for what you don't have?	❑	❑
• Have you avoided making any negative remarks about yourself?	❑	❑
• Does your letter sound sincere and not overly flattering?	❑	❑
• Have you avoided slang terms?	❑	❑
• Have you removed any words that sound pompous or old-fashioned?	❑	❑
• Is your letter grammatically correct?	❑	❑
• Have you checked carefully for spelling errors?	❑	❑
• Have you shown your final draft to two people and sought their opinion?	❑	❑
• Have you arranged for your letter to be typed and laser-printed?	❑	❑

The Last Step

When you send your letter, make sure it is the original, not a photocopy. You should keep a hard copy in a file as well as one on computer. This will become part of your Job Search Diary, containing letters you receive and copies of those you send.

The appearance of your covering letter is as important as its content. You should avoid smudges or typing mistakes. If you overlook these points, you could spoil your chances of being successful, even though you have worked hard at making your job application interesting.

Your job application letter must be typed. It will be read by people who are used to reading typewritten letters and reports. You may think your handwriting is easy to read, but others may not.

A good way of producing several job application letters is to use a word processor or personal computer. If you don't have one yourself, you may know someone who has access to one. On such a machine it is easy and quick to produce many letters, only requiring you to make those changes necessary to suit each application.

Use good quality paper for your letters; it shows the reader that you take pride in what you do. Remember that when you are looking for a job, you want everything you do to make a good impression. It is worth the time, money and energy to use good quality stationery.

Avoid folding your letter. Buy envelopes that allow your A4 pages to remain flat; and pay the (small) extra postage so that your application reaches the employer unfolded and looking as tidy as when you completed it.

Checklist 4 (Complete prior to mailing your job application)

	Yes	No
• Have you signed your application letter?	❑	❑
• Is the envelope correctly addressed, with your name and address on the back?	❑	❑
• Is the font style the same as you have used for your résumé?	❑	❑
• Is the envelope big enough so that you don't have to fold your letter?	❑	❑
• Have you avoided perfumed or coloured stationery?	❑	❑
• Does your letter fit on one page?	❑	❑
• Is your name printed below your signature?	❑	❑
• Have you kept a copy for your Job Search Diary?	❑	❑
• Have you noted the date of mailing in your Job Search Diary?	❑	❑
• Is your résumé stapled in the top left hand corner to your letter?	❑	❑

Your Job Search Diary

Success often comes as a result of thoroughness. Job-searching requires three things: organisation, imagination and persistence. Applying each could help you reduce the time you may spend job hunting.

I have designed a book, *Your Job Search Organiser*, for this purpose. It includes space for you to enter all the information relating to each job application you send, as well as telephone numbers, interview appointments and so on.

Writing down a summary of information you receive will stop you from confusing information about one employer with another.

Keep a record of what you have done and dates when you expect action from others. Write the key points discussed at the interview and the names of people you met.

Carry a notebook with you during your job-searching activities. Record information and reminder notes to yourself about things you have learned and committed to do.

Write up your Job Search Diary each day. With your Job Search Diary kept up-to-date, the danger of mixing up information, confusing facts about one job prospect with another or failing to follow-up on time is substantially reduced.

Suggested Layout for Your Letters

Home Address
Street
Suburb or Town & Postcode

Tel: (Home and Work)
Fax: (if you   )
Email: (have one)

Date

Name
Job Title
Company Name
Postal Address, including
Suburb or Town and Postcode

Dear

Body of Letter

In the samples which follow, only the body of the letter appears. Please refer to this suggested layout to ensure that all the relevant contact information is included. Note that the words line up on the left.

Yours sincerely

Your Signature

Your Name

6 Sample Letters

Easy-to-Find Index

Pre-Application Research

Applications

Follow-Up

Job Search Conclusion

Thanking Job Search Helpers

Pre-Application Research

Request for Research Interview

> A few moments with you would benefit me immensely. Your industry appears to be the one most likely to make the best use of my skills. An appreciation of the problems which you experience would help me to validate whether this career direction is sound for me.
>
> I've prepared well for such a discussion and won't take up more than twenty minutes of your time.
>
> If it is convenient for you, please call me on (02) 6265 3991 any day before noon.

Networking Request for Research Interview

> Sylvia James suggested that I contact you about my interest in Human Resource Management. She said that you are one of the best people to talk to concerning careers in Human Resources.
>
> I am leaving my current position after seven years' experience and increasing responsibilities in HR. I am especially interested in working with a large private firm. However, before I venture further into the job market, I want to benefit from the experience and knowledge of others in the field who can advise me on opportunities for someone with my qualifications.
>
> Perhaps we could meet briefly some time during the next two weeks to discuss my career plans? I have several questions which I believe you could clarify. I will call your office next week to schedule a meeting time.
>
> I look forward to discussing my plans with you.

Thankyou Following Research Interview

> Your advice was most helpful in clarifying my questions on careers in Advertising. I am now reworking my résumé and have included many of your thoughtful suggestions. I will send you a copy next week.
>
> Thank you for taking time from your busy schedule to see me. I will keep in contact and follow through on your suggestion to see Ms Baker about opportunities with XYZ Company.

Letter to Referee with Résumé

As you may be aware, I am seeking new growth opportunities in the field of Engineering and request your help as a referee.

Since I have not seen you recently, I have enclosed a résumé updating my activities. Should you hear of any opportunities, I would appreciate your letting me know.

If a job lead develops to the point of reference checking, I will fill you in on the position prior to anyone contacting you.

My sincere appreciation for your help and cooperation.

Networking Letter to Personal Contact

I'm writing for your help. Through my enclosed résumé I am looking for a new position in Sales Management. As I have done in the past, I'm the person who can set new sales records in the future. This could be for a company you know. Your help in providing leads to organisations I might suit would be greatly appreciated. I will phone you in a few days.

Thank you

With best regards

PS   (Add a statement of a personal nature)

(Note: This letter should be signed using your first name)

Applications

Response to Advertisements — Private Sector Employer

Re: Your Advertisement in The Australian 8 February 1998

I have initiated and managed all your seven specified Marketing Research requirements as an operating manager and as a consultant, producing the following results:

- Turned a long-term loss into the first profit for a product line of 100 seafoods

- Established profitable market in industry for a household chemical firm

- Laid out five-year program to increase sales by $1.9 million for aluminium producer

- Programmed sales expansions from under $2 million to over $8 million, realised by two national brand manufacturers

My formal training included Marketing and Research at the Graduate School of Business, after graduating from the University of Melbourne.

I would like to go over the direct applications of my experience to your needs during a meeting with you.

Response to Advertisements — Recruitment Consultants

Re: 'Advertising Career Opportunity' - The West Australian, 10/3/98

Your client requires a very competent person to act as Sales Executive.

I can offer the following attributes:
- Resourceful market strategist and tactician
- Accomplished salesperson
- Astute media researcher, analyst and planner
- Excellent communication and people management skills

My enclosed résumé provides a detailed outline of my experience and an insight into my expertise and diligence in pursuit of commercial goals.

I would like to meet you soon. Please telephone me on 9406 9315 to arrange such a discussion.

Response to Advertisements — Public Sector Employer

I wish to apply for the position of Supervisor—Adult Migrant Education Service, Position No. 98/136.

If successful in my application, I would be able to apply the following transferable knowledge and skills:

- Twenty years' experience in teaching adults

- Tertiary qualifications in adult education and applied linguistics

- The management, needs assessment and coordination of the work of others in education settings

- A record of developmental initiatives in new learning methods

- The design, planning, coordination and evaluation of English language programs

- Extensive practical experience both personally and through the supervision of student teachers in TESOL

- Familiarity in the workplace of the need for, the difficulties and awareness of, Equal Employment Opportunity facilities

My detailed credentials supporting this application are attached.

Unsolicited Application to Employers

As I think you would appreciate, success in achieving a career objective takes more than having the relevant qualifications, experience and a good past performance record. A flexible attitude and adaptability with regard to type of work, position level and location are very important. A conscientious and determined approach to carrying out assignments is also helpful. These are the qualities I want to emphasise in my approach to gaining employment with your organisation.

My primary interest is to be employed within the Financial Services industry. The enclosed résumé shows the energy I have applied to obtaining qualifications and developing readily transferable skills.

I would like to meet you, or your nominated staff member, to discuss this further.

Unsolicited Application to Employers

> My research indicates that your company is likely to be interested in employing a person with a fundamentally practical approach to computer operations, systems development and client service.
>
> Waiting for the 'right' recruitment advertisement to appear doesn't suit my nature and eagerness to progress my career. So, I am approaching you with the conviction I can offer the following:
>
> - Broad practical experience in an in-house installation and a vigorous customer-service bureau
>
> - Thorough training in Information Systems basics
>
> - Ability to work efficiently and effectively with others
>
> - An enthusiasm for maintaining control over a number of tasks at once
>
> - An awareness that I have much to learn, in addition to my very useful experience and training
>
> My enclosed résumé briefly outlines the activities from which I have learned the meaning of hard work and developed my attitude towards working conscientiously for my employer.
>
> I would like to meet you to explore your needs in greater detail and where I may be of assistance.

Unsolicited Application to Recruitment Consultants

> In the course of your search activities you may have a requirement for a person accomplished in marketing in the Financial Services sector.
>
> My career has covered responsible positions with several companies, including four years with my current employer. A review of my enclosed résumé will demonstrate to you a record of increasing responsibility and a sample of my commercial achievements.
>
> If it appears that my qualifications meet a client company's current needs, I would be happy to discuss my background with you in greater depth.

Search for Temporary or Freelance Work

> I am seeking a position as a Credit Officer, Part-Time, within an Accounts Department. My enclosed résumé provides you with many details of my background, skills and training experiences.
>
> If any of your clients has a recruitment need in this field, I would be keen to discuss their career opportunities with you.
>
> Please contact me on (03) 9384 1947 to arrange a time to meet.

Unsolicited Application to Recruitment Consultants

> I am confidentially exploring new employment opportunities in the field of Accounting and believe you might be interested in assisting me.
>
> I am hoping that you will be in contact with employers to whom my particular skills and capabilities will appeal.
>
> Please call me on (03) 9559 3481 to answer any questions you may have or to arrange a meeting to discuss career possibilities.

To Prospective Employer Following Network Referral

> David White has suggested that I write to you about seeking an entry-level management position in the field of Marketing. For the past two years I have been in management training with the State Bank.
>
> During that period my training has been very extensive in both operations and consumer loans. In addition, I have been involved with special assignments, such as:
>
> • Account Profitability Analysis
> • New Accounts Set Up/Introduction
> • Customer Information File
>
> I also believe that my Degree in Business Administration with emphasis on marketing can be utilised effectively by your organisation.
>
> I would appreciate the opportunity of a personal interview with you. I will call you within the next ten days to set up an interview date.

To Prospective Employer Following Article in Magazine or Newspaper

In a recent edition of *Construction News*, your firm was featured as an innovative designer of shopping centres. Since my philosophies in exterior design seem very compatible with yours, you could be interested in my qualifications and experience as an employee.

Shopping centres have significant appeal to women, so, as a young woman, I feel that I can provide a variety of profitable creative ideas for your organisation.

Some of my accomplishments are:

- Recently completed the design concept for an $8 million shopping complex designed for high quality specialty shops

- Received the Max Reid Award for Design Excellence for the innovative design of an indoor recreational complex

Your organisation could provide the challenge and creative stimulation I am seeking.

Application Following Retrenchment

You may have a need for a person capable of acting efficiently without the need for close supervision, who has a thorough understanding of training methods and employee development activities.

As you may be aware, my current employer is retrenching and my position will be terminated at the end of this month. After you have assessed my credentials outlined in the enclosed résumé, please contact me to arrange a time to meet. I am able to meet during or outside business hours.

7   Follow-Up Letters

Importance of Follow-Up Letters

After a job interview, applicants wait for the good or bad news. It is no fun sitting by the telephone or fax, or marking time, anxious for each mail delivery. A follow-up letter, expressing your appreciation for the opportunity of an interview, can achieve the following for you:

- It reiterates your interest in the job and gives you an edge over other applicants.
- It gives you a second chance to communicate your best feature that is relevant to the job.
- It shows that you are still confident about handling the job.
- It keeps your name prominent in the recipient's mind.
- It can help to speed up action on the part of the recipient.

Most applicants neglect this opportunity. A polite expression of gratitude could decide selection in your favour, particularly if you show that you remember a significant fact from the interview. Chances are you will be one of the very few who were interviewed who are thoughtful enough to send a follow-up letter.

If, as sometimes happens, the interviewer is left with only vague impressions of dozens of applicants, the person may remember you better through this action.

Tone

Be conscious of the tone you use in your letter. Every time we speak or write, we are dealing with 'tone of voice', as well as meaning—and quite often our tone has the greater effect.

The first thing to do before you write this letter is to think about who the likely receiver is and about his or her outlook. The next step is to be quite clear about why you are writing. When you have your objective clear, a better letter will result.

Follow-up letters are often very difficult to phrase. However, you are no longer writing to a stranger. An exception to this is a follow-up letter in the case of receiving no response to your job application to gain an interview.

Purpose of Follow-Up Letters

The sample letters which follow will help you to write letters for a number of purposes:

1. To encourage action when you have received no reply to your job application;
2. To thank an employer after an interview;
3. To accept an employment offer;
4. To delay acceptance of an employment offer;
5. To decline an employment offer;
6. To thank those who have helped you in your job search.

Checklist (Complete when you have drafted your follow-up letters)

✓

Yes No

- Have you thanked the interviewer for an interesting and informative interview? ❑ ❑

- Does your letter indicate that you have remembered an important fact learnt at the interview about your prospective employer? ❑ ❑

- Have you been able to remind the interviewer of something the person liked about your application? ❑ ❑

- Have you included any important points about yourself that you neglected to mention at the interview? (Ideally, you did raise all the important points during your meeting.) ❑ ❑

- Have you referred to their needs rather than yours? ❑ ❑

- Have you shown enthusiasm for the job in your letter? ❑ ❑

- Have you clearly expressed your interest in working for this employer? ❑ ❑

- Have you avoided asking for an answer to your job application by a certain date? ❑ ❑

- Have you avoided sounding annoyed at not learning the result of the interview? ❑ ❑

- Is your letter brief and does it fit onto one page? ❑ ❑

- Are the interviewer's name and job title spelt correctly? ❑ ❑

- Have you included your contact information? ❑ ❑

- Have you set your follow-up letter out correctly? (See page 169 for our suggested layout) ❑ ❑

Application Progress Enquiry

When writing for such a purpose, consider following the structure shown in the following model letter and sample.

Open politely by saying you think your original application may have been lost in the mail. Don't accuse the receiver of neglecting you through not replying. You should also avoid expressing your annoyance or indicating any desperation for a job.

State the date that the original letter and résumé were mailed. Comment that a further copy of your résumé is enclosed.

Highlight a significant claim of yours for consideration that is relevant to the specific job or industry. Mention anything new that you have learnt about the industry or this organisation.

Request an interview, giving times that are convenient for you and including your telephone number.

Follow-Up When No Reply Received to Job Application

My letter and résumé were mailed to your organisation on 9 February 1998. The enquiry concerned employment opportunities in your scientific laboratories.

Mail delays may have caused communications between us to have been lost. Just in case this has occurred, a copy of my résumé is enclosed.

Naturally, I am anxious to learn of any progress with my application. Your firm was selected as a very appealing one from those I researched when preparing for my current search for an appropriate employer.

I am available for interview any afternoon after 3.30 pm. Do let me know which day is convenient for you by telephoning 9381 3920 (work) or 9839 2917 (home) after 7 pm.

Interview Follow-Up Letters

Just a brief note to thank you for the interest you have shown in my employment application and for the information provided at our discussion on Monday. Seeing Berkeley's from the inside has made the career opportunity even more attractive to me.

I have located a copy of the Government report on your industry which you mentioned. It certainly has improved my knowledge.

After our meeting I have considered carefully the energy and ability necessary for success with your company and am confident I can provide them.

Our interview on 14 October has increased my enthusiasm for joining Nationwide Industries.

The position you outlined appears to offer a real opportunity to apply my learning and to learn more. My extensive project work in statistics should help me with the problems that your Market Research Department experiences. I am delaying other job searching enquiries until I hear from you.

I also enjoyed meeting the employees in the section and discussing the tasks and problems.

Do let me know as soon as you can whether I am fortunate enough to be offered the position.

Thank you for our interview last Friday. After carefully considering your comments, I am very sure that I would like to work for Associated Planning Engineers Pty Ltd.

I also enjoyed talking with Mr Harold Jones about the tasks and problems of the drafting section. I certainly would benefit by learning from a man of his ability and experience. I did neglect to tell him that my work experience program last year involved working in the drafting section of the Department of Main Roads.

Do let me know, as soon as you are able to, whether I will be offered a position.

Job Search Conclusion

Delaying Acceptance of an Employment Offer

Thank you very much for offering me the position of Sales Consultant. I am very pleased with your decision and assure you of my serious interest in your organisation.

I am scheduled to attend three more interviews before next Wednesday. So that I may make the best possible decision, I would appreciate your allowing me a brief time to fulfil these obligations and consider your offer.

I expect to give you my decision by 20 March, if this meets with your approval. If, however, you need my decision before that time, please contact me on 8363 5414.

Accepting an Employment Offer

> Your offer of employment has been received following our discussion. I am pleased to accept this appointment. The terms and conditions you have proposed are also acceptable to me.
>
> I look forward to contributing to the tasks and challenges you described when I commence employment on 8 September.

Declining an Employment Offer

> I am replying to the offer of employment which you have made to me on behalf of your firm. I appreciate both the offer and the time taken to introduce me to the vacancy, your procedures and the company in general.
>
> Unfortunately, I am already committed to another employer and am unable to accept your offer.

Declining an Employment Offer

> I would like to thank you for the warm reception you and your staff have shown me on the occasions when we have met recently. With this in mind, it is difficult for me to advise you that I am declining your employment offer.
>
> Should the need arise, however, I would very much like the chance to meet with you again.

Declining an Employment Offer

> After meeting you and other members of the Jones Advertising team, it is difficult to turn down your offer received today. Important decisions in my career transition are harder than I anticipated.
>
> I am honoured by your offer of employment. I must, however, decline because I have reasoned that starting with another firm is a more appropriate match for my learning needs and experience contribution. Thank you for your time and consideration with my application.

Thanking Job Search Helpers

You have been successful in your job search, but there is one more important task—that is to write a thankyou letter to those who have helped you.

Sending a thankyou letter—similar to those which follow—to people who have given you advice or acted as your referee is an important courtesy and will be appreciated. Also, you may be doing yourself a favour if you need their help again later on. Not every job works out to the satisfaction of the successful applicant.

If you have been granted an interview by a prospective employer, it is especially important at this stage to send a thankyou letter advising them that you are no longer job searching.

Thankyou Letter to Referee

I am very pleased to be able to let you know that my job search has ended. My new position is Purchasing Officer for the construction company, Trihard Pty Ltd.

I have been fortunate in being able to choose from several offers. This has been due in some part to your efforts—describing to me various career alternatives and acting as my referee. I am very grateful for your advice and activities on my behalf.

Many thanks.

Thankyou Letter to Referee

My new job with Smith Bros. Pty Ltd starts next month. Your thoughtful recommendation helped me obtain this employment offer.

Many thanks for your help.

Thankyou Letter to Information Provider

Thank you for all your answers to my many questions at our meeting on 8 November. Your insights and advice about the job role of financial analyst helped me focus better in my job targeting. Your emphasis on presentation skills prompted me to enrol quickly in a short skills building course on it, which I have added to my résumé.

Consequently, I am delighted to let you know that I start with Amber Bros next Monday in such a position. I will let you know how my rejuvenated career unfolds. Again, many thanks for your contribution.

8   Student Résumé Writing

Students usually consider education their most important qualification. You should be careful, however, not to imply that those results are your only qualification for employment. People who seek to employ students look beyond academic qualifications when determining the suitability of applicants.

Very few of us score excellent results in examinations. Student job seekers often make the mistake of thinking that employers are interested in hiring only those lucky few. Employers really seek a wide range of qualities, not just those measured by examinations. A student may have done well in other activities, or may have gained knowledge from many different learning experiences. The art of successful job seeking is to work out which of your activities and experiences—in and out of classes and lectures—have given you qualities that are valuable to employers.

All students have something of value to offer employers. Some have the ability to analyse problems, to look at issues fairly and thoughtfully; others can see another's point of view or are able to communicate information and ideas. All these skills are useful in the world of work.

You could be selected for an interview on the basis of :
- part-time or casual employment;
- community service and voluntary work;
- sports activities;
- hobbies;
- vocational interest or career guidance results;
- travel experience;
- positions of responsibility held in clubs or societies;
- work experience.

In every job, whatever its name, you need to communicate with other people, act responsibly, take care in carrying out job tasks and try each day to do better than yesterday. You can show prospective employers that you have gained these qualities in ways other than exam results. It could be through involvement in sporting teams, hobbies, special projects, positions of responsibility or the careful way you have handled the money that you have earned.

Your educational record demonstrates that you are mentally alert, have the ability to apply your intelligence to solving problems and can think logically. The transcript of your subject results, however, is just not sufficient, even if it contains consistently high grades such as credits and distinctions. To be an effective job searcher you need to design a complete résumé—one that records a lot more about you than your educational success.

As a student you face the special challenge of composing and designing a job application that clearly differentiates you from the many other students competing for similar jobs. The sample résumés and covering letters which follow will help you with this task. Use the checklists for résumés and for application letters to prepare your drafts and final copies.

Work Experience Visits

You may have spent some time with an employer on a work experience visit arranged by your school careers adviser or during vacation from secondary or tertiary studies. Perhaps you kept a diary of what you learnt and felt about the job tasks you did or observed. Reading over your notes now could help you to find useful information to enter in your résumé. Remember, the employer is not only interested in whether or not you have had work experience, but could also be very interested in your comments on what you feel you learnt.

If you didn't keep a diary, spend time now writing down your thoughts about your work experiences. List the tasks you did while you were with the employer. Add a list of the tasks you observed other people doing. Write a sentence or two that sum up the main things you learnt. Record a particular accomplishment during this work experience of which you are quite proud. Look over your notes and select two or three points to highlight in your résumé.

Unpaid Working Experience

This often tells an employer more about your capabilities than your paid working experience. It may include work experience gained through school programs, volunteer work and community service tasks in which you have been involved. Record the name of the organisation that you worked for and the results of your work.

Practical Work Experience

Under this heading you should include all your paid working experience in vacation, part-time and casual jobs. Do not dismiss any of it as too trivial or short-lived. Everything you have done is of value here.

You may be surprised to see how much you have gained from your work experiences. What have you learnt through jobs you have had?

In every activity involving work, you have:
- gained experiences that will help you understand or quickly learn the duties of a new job;
- learnt to adapt to other people and to different tasks;
- learnt to adjust to the world of work;
- learnt to be punctual;
- learnt about working hard.

You may also have:
- handled employer's equipment with care;
- handled other people's money responsibly.

Awards and Prizes

So far you have considered your working experiences and the skills developed from them. But there's more to a person than that. Every employer also needs to learn about your other skills and achievements.

As a result of your years at school and perhaps at a tertiary education institution, you have probably received special recognition, awards or honours. You may also have been applauded for extra-curricular (out-of-school) activities, sports, hobbies and interests. Include scholarships, certificates or medals in this section. These experiences will also have taught you a great deal.

Other Talents and Skills

This section of a résumé gives you a chance to list special talents and skills you have developed. These may be musical, athletic, mechanical or artistic. They may include skills in typing, languages, drawing, etc. As you think about your hobbies and interests, you may realise that you have gained useful skills. Often such information can show employers how your talents could be best used as their employee.

Education and Training

Record the basic facts of your educational achievements. You can arrange the information in a way that best represents how you performed in your studies. List any training programs or courses of instruction that you have taken part in. (Public speaking, drama, peer group counselling, etc.)

What to Look for in the Sample Résumés

You may feel that some of the applicants have been bold or over-assertive in the samples résumés; and that you would not be prepared to use a similar style. It is important, however, to be positive, brief and confident when writing about your skills and abilities.

No résumé or letter written by another person is going to fit your needs exactly. You will, however, benefit by examining the samples phrase by phrase as you construct your own.

Use the résumés as a guide only. If you like the sound of a statement or phrase, underline or highlight it. You may wish to use it in your own résumé and change the words to suit your own situation. If you would like to use any phrases in these samples, re-word them to match your own style. In this way you will be able to ensure they match the rest of your résumé.

Remember that a well-designed résumé should emphasise your main assets and so make the best possible impression. It's a word picture of your life to date and an important key to your future. Make sure your résumé reflects everything that you have accomplished which is relevant and shows that you are likely to be able to do the job you seek.

Notice how the headings for different sections have been chosen carefully. Note also how the headings and sections have been positioned so that each one is easy to read.

REMINDER! One more time

Take a pen or a highlighter and, as you read through each and every résumé in this Guide. Mark where you observe:

- a layout that appeals to you;
- innovative use of section headings;
- information which matches (or is similar to) yours;
- words which you could adapt.

Only then, start the first draft of your résumé.

9 Sample Résumés for Students

Easy-to-Find Index

Résumés for Students

Checklists for Your Résumé

When you have prepared the first draft of your résumé, refer to the following checklists to ensure you have put together all the information in the best possible format:

RESUME OF:

LOUISE FAIRCLOUGH

84 Samson Street
NARRABEEN 2109   Phone: (02) 9901 1176

JOB OBJECTIVE

Seeking part-time casual employment on Saturdays and/or Sundays in a hospitality or tourism service operation.

MAIN CAPABILITY AREAS

- Work experience in tourism at ID Tours 1997
- Proved to be a team-player, a responsible, hardworking and enthusiastic employee at Macdonald's 1997
- Baby-sitting since the age of 12 for younger sisters and neighbourhood families
- Demonstrated a keen understanding of all subjects in High School
- Developed commendable study habits proving dedication and enthusiasm
- Second in Form in Year 9 & 10 English
- Top five in Year 10 Science (advanced class)
- Advanced Mathematics

EDUCATIONAL ATTAINMENT'S

Have accomplished four years of high school and am continuing to complete Years 11 and 12

Participated in debating for school in 1995 and in school sporting events.

School netball team

Have attended a wide variety of schools and have coped well, giving me flexibility and the ability to easily adapt

High Schools attended are St Alban's College, Northwood NSW and Ascot College, Fremantle WA. Received good reports from both schools

SPECIAL ACHIEVEMENTS

Completed School Certificate and all exams in Year 10 1997

Performed well in Year 10 Trial moderator and School Certificate 1997

Maintained place in top five in English and Science Years 8, 9 and 10

Produced high marks in all assessments during Years 8-10

Certificate of excellence in Drama for 1996

PERSONAL DEVELOPMENT ACTIVITIES

Achieved credit awards in state-wide Science competition in Years 8, 9 and 10.

Provided own money through part-time job at Macdonald's

Award for Excellence in Drama 1997

Second in Moderator Trial exam for English

Louise Fairclough

PEOPLE WHO KNOW ME WELL

Mrs Beth Downer
25 View Street, Narrabeen
Phone: (02) 9901 9320

Mrs Diana Cusack
95 Habourside Parade, Narrabeen
Phone: (02) 9972 9105

MORE FACTS ABOUT ME

Born 15 October 1982

Am Australian citizen and have lived in Saudi Arabia, Perth, Sydney

Demonstrated ability to adapt to new situations and adjust easily to change

Attended drama school 1993

Enjoy reading, writing, drama, netball

Travelled to Europe, Britain, North and South America

Excellent health

Participated in Red Shield Appeal 1997

REFERENCES AVAILABLE ON REQUEST

LEANNE HENRY
Tel: (02) 9572 9153
or leave message (02) 9291 4398

OBJECTIVE
To achieve part-time or contract employment over next twelve months in Hospitality industry whilst continuing to study part-time at University of Sydney in an industry-related course. Flexible attitude towards hours of work.

EMPLOYMENT EXPERIENCES
- Tyrrells Wines, Chatswood: Wine Promotions part-time from Sept 1997
- Cricketers' Arms, Surry Hills: Bartender part-time from Sept 1995 - June 1997
- Wentworth Bar Bartender part-time from June to Dec 1996
- Rag & Famish Hotel, North Sydney: Bartender Public and Main Bars plus Restaurant part-time from Jan to June 1996
- UNISYS Australia Limited: Telephone Customer Service from Nov 1994 to Feb 1995
- Reark Market Research: part-time over 3 months
- Worklife Options Publishing Company, Sydney: Receptionist, stock selection, dispatch, banking, basic bookkeeping, part-time over two and a half years

SKILLS DEVELOPMENT
Commercial:
- Completed Metropolitan Business College, Autumn 1994. Award: Certificate of Office Skills (Bookkeeping, Computers, Word Perfect 5.1 & Word for Windows, Business Communications). Present typing speed of 50 wpm
- Completed Alex Beaumont's Cocktails and Mixed Drinks Bar Course, Jan 1994. 90% Pass mark

Teamwork, Creativity & Innovation:
- Elected Delegate to National Union of Students
- Elected Co-Editor of Student Newspaper
- University Co-Environment Officer 1997
- Environment Committee 1995-97
- Vice President Sydney University Greens 1997
- Participated Students and Sustainability Conference 1995-97
- Member, Women's Collective
- SRC Representative, 68th Council 1996
- SRC Co-Welfare Officer, 1996
- SRC Co-Housing Officer, 1996
- Active Participant, Students Environmental Activist Network (SEAN)
- Committee Member, Sydney University Bookshop Committee

SENIOR SCHOOL STUDIES
HSC (Oct 1993) St Clair High School
Awards:
- Bronze and Silver Duke of Edinburgh Scheme
- High Distinction Australian Speech Communication Association

PERSONAL
Born 12 March 1976 ... Australian citizen. ... Hold an unrestricted drivers licence. References on request

Résumé of:

SIMON MITCHELL

Tel: (02) 4757 3829
82 Henry Parkes Drive, Penrith 2750

CAREER OBJECTIVE	To achieve a high standard of performance in my chosen trade as an Electrician and complete my training and TAFE studies diligently.
SUMMARY	Throughout my teenage years I have sought to develop my practical skills at school, in hobbies and casual employment in electrical and electronic activities. Am confident that my chosen career is appropriate for me.
SENIOR SCHOOL STUDIES	HSC (Oct 1997) Penrith High School 2 Unit level: English, Maths, Physics, Economics, Geography; 1 Unit General Studies. Completed Computer Studies Year 11
USEFUL WORK EXPERIENCES	• Assisted in the extensive rewiring and power system design within two domestic homes during 1996/97 • Initiated and carried out my own lawn mowing contracting business for twelve months' accumulative time • Undertaken several house renovations
WORK EXPERIENCE REPORT EXTRACTS	'Simon earned an Excellent Rating in all categories while engaged in Electrical work. He has tremendous potential in the electrical trade; very advanced in technique for one so young.' (D Woods) 'Simon was always on time, neat and tidy, with an eager interest in work. His cooperation was always given; very pleasant impression and will be an asset as an employee.' (Video Rentals Pty Ltd, 1996)
TEAMWORK	• Representative for school in Rugby (First XV 1996), Athletics, Swimming, Relays • Camp Leadership assignments
OTHER USEFUL FACTS ABOUT ME	• Awarded Certificate by GEC Australia Ltd for Talent • Completed successfully Driver Awareness Course 1997
REFEREES	Derek Woods Margaret Jamieson, Teacher / Counsellor Electrical Contractor Penrith High School Tel: (02) 4757 6028 Tel: (02) 4757 3911
PERSONAL	Born 30 November 1979 ... verified my career direction choice with a professional career counsellor in Sept 1997 (Report available) ... in my own income-earning endeavours and assisting others in their small businesses have learnt much about customer service, cash handling, efficiency and craftsmanship

Résumé of:

DANIEL CROSSING
Telephone (03) 5341 2405

CAREER OBJECTIVE:

To develop a career in my chosen field where I can work to the fullest of my ability and use the skills I have acquired, such as preventative and emergency maintenance, problem solving and general fabrication work. I feel these skills, plus the ease with which I communicate with people, would help to develop my expertise even further.

FORMAL QUALIFICATIONS:

* Completed and eligible for indentures - 24 Dec 1997
* Achieved three years' Technical Education at Portland TAFE College
* Attained successful results in all three years of my Technical Education
* Awarded a Trades Certificate in Welding Trades at the completion of my Apprenticeship
* Obtained School Certificate, Portland High School, 1993

PRACTICAL EXPERIENCE:

Portland Cement Limited
Commenced employment in January 1994
* Trained and supervised in a Production Workshop
* Worked in several emergency maintenance situations
* Participated in designing and fabrication of equipment in the Works Drawing Office
* Unsupervised work and directing others played a substantial part in the last year of my Apprenticeship
* Obtained experience with a wide range of mechanical equipment, e.g. Radial Drills, Presses, Coal and Limestone Reclaimers
Prior to Portland Cement, employed as a labourer to bricklayers and carpenters

HOBBIES AND INTERESTS:

* Received membership to Portland Sports Club and was member of the Portland Football Club for several years
* Enjoy restoring old cars and learning how they work
* Planned and organised arrangements for several holidays for friends and myself

REFEREES:

* Mark Spicer	* Philip McWilliam
Manager	Assistant Manager
Portland Cement	Cut-Price Supermarket
Tel: 5241 3922	Tel: 5241 8388

PERSONAL DATA:

Address: 58 Hunter Street, Portland 3305
Enjoy the company of other people and prepared to relocate if necessary

Résumé of:

BRETT JAMES
Tel: (02) 9389 3752
Unit 18, 682 New South Head Road, Rose Bay 2029

CAREER OBJECTIVE

To apply diligently my training in commercial practices and finance leading to a career in the Financial Services sector, such as a Merchant Bank or related environment

TERTIARY QUALIFICATIONS

Currently studying (final year) Bachelor of Business degree University of Technology, Sydney, majoring in Finance.
24 subjects completed: Corporate Finance, Advanced Corporate Finance, Accounting I, II & IV, Economy & Society I, II & III, Communications I & II, Quantitative Methods I, Advanced Quantitative Methods, etc.
Achieved 3 Distinctions, 9 Credits
Remaining subjects: Accounting V, Security Analysis & Portfolio Management, Security Market Regulation, Modern Finance Theory, International Finance and Corporate Strategy

SENIOR SCHOOL STUDIES

HSC 1995, Waverley College
Subjects: Economics, Maths, English, Physics, Modern History, General Studies. Top 10% Maths & Economics

USEFUL WORK EXPERIENCE

- Options Broker: Sydney Futures Exchange (4 months)
- Casual work experience: Australian Stock Exchange
- Clerical: District Nursing Service
- Market Research: Telephone Interviewer, Marketing Survey Centre
- Bar work: King William Hotel

OTHER USEFUL FACTS ABOUT ME

- Am computer literate and used to software applications
- Found employment at the Stock and Futures Exchanges particularly informative and useful
- Member of UTS Business Society
- Member of AISEC
- Participated in Intervarsity Ski competition
- Captained a number of school Rugby Union Teams
- Enjoy Tennis, Squash, Golf, Reading, Music and Travel

REFEREES

Mr J E Frederickson
Chartered Accountant
Williams and Phillips
Tel: (B) 9262 1995

Dr P W Marks
Professor of Medicine
St Vincent's Hospital
Tel: (B) 9212 3777

PERSONAL

Born 7 April 1977 ... Single ... enjoy meeting people and working in a team environment ... excellent health ... no stranger to hard work

KATHRYN HEMPENSTALL

EMPLOYMENT OBJECTIVE

To work in the field of Wildlife with special consideration for their preservation and well-being. To rehabilitate animals to their natural environment where suitable. Particularly interested in improving the relationship between people and animals.

EDUCATIONAL ACHIEVEMENTS

* Successfully completed Higher School Certificate in 1994 at Benton College with a good result in Biology

* Currently completing a Bachelor of Arts in Humanities at Griffith University

* Seeking part-time or correspondence course in Park Management

USEFUL WORKING EXPERIENCE

* Completed a work experience program in Year 10 with a veterinary surgeon, continued occasional work with a vet over the past five years

* Being involved in all aspects of animal care, handling and husbandry on the family farm has provided practical experience in dealing with animals

* Waitressing at a large functions restaurant in Brisbane has taught me responsibility and a greater awareness of dealing with people

SPECIAL LEARNING EXPERIENCES

* Living and schooling in four countries has given me flexibility to adapt to new situations and adjust easily to change

HOBBIES AND INTERESTS

* Camping and bushwalking
* Horse riding
* Photography and design
* Raising young animals
* Woodwork

PERSONAL INFORMATION

* Enjoy outdoor activities and prepared to work hard and with dedication

* Address: 'Keywood', Nora Road, Quilpie 4480

* Telephone: (07) 4342 9357

Referees will be provided when requested

KAY WATKINS

87 Wunda Street, Narrabundah ACT 2604   Tel: (02) 6275.0826 (Home)

CAREER OBJECTIVE	To achieve employment success and career progress as a Corporate Lawyer.
TERTIARY EDUCATION ACHIEVEMENTS	• GRADUATED from the Faculty of Law, Australian National University in November 1997 following 4 years' attendance including extended studies in Revenue Law, Industrial & Commercial Property, Conveyancing &Public International Law • DEVELOPED personal independence by living at Burton College during studies and actively contributing to Committee work for a variety of endeavours
EXPERIENCES FROM WHICH I HAVE GAINED MUCH	• Temporary employment within the Fast Food business, David Jones Department Store, Federal Electoral Office (Poll Clerk, Assistant Presiding Officer), the offices of two Barristers-at-Law and a Member of the NSW Medical Disciplinary Tribunal • Regular part-time employment over past five years as Receptionist / Secretary / Bookkeeper to busy Obstetrician and Gynaecologist Medical practice • Instructor for Lifesaving Association of NSW; Volunteer work at Woden Valley Hospital (Nursery Section) and UNICEF • Earning the Duke of Edinburgh's Awards—Bronze and Silver and progressing to Award of Merit Level in Lifesaving • Secondary education was completed at SCEGGS Darlinghurst from which I gained a sound academic training, combined with successful participation in many sports and involvement in personal development activities ranging from Debating Teams, Charities, Drama and Investment Clubs
PEOPLE WHO KNOW ME WELL	• Mr Vic Masterton Former Vice-Principal Burton College, ANU Telephone: (02) 6273 1733 • Dr Bruce Thompson Medical Administrator Woden Valley Hospital Telephone: (02) 6267 4911
PERSONAL DATA	Date of Birth: 14 February 1975. Employment experiences have taught me a lot about dealing with customers and clients, carrying out tasks conscientiously and securing the cooperation of others. Further studies are planned subject to the requirements of my employer and the career path available. Believe my determination, interpersonal skills and ability to work hard will return well my employer's investment in further training.

Résumé of:

TERRY HOWARD

37 Normanton Way, HYDE PARK SA 5061
Telephone: (08) 8382 7108

OBJECTIVE

To apply my university training and associated practical experience to develop my career within Civil Engineering and, in particular, my understanding of Concrete Technology

AVAILABILITY FOR EMPLOYMENT: Within two weeks of employment acceptance ... prepared to relocate subject to nature of career opportunity

TERTIARY QUALIFIED

*   Graduate BEng (Civil) Majoring in Structures, University of Adelaide School of Civil and Mining Engineering

*   Thesis: "Effects of fly ash on ternary systems of ordinary Portland cement, granulated blast furnace slag and fly ash"

*   Practical Training Report: Researched, formulated and compiled at Department of Marine and Harbours 1995/96. Available for employers' review. Awarded High Distinction 89%

*   Undergraduate Record: Credit awards in Industrial Relations, Structural Behaviour and other subjects

PERSONAL DEVELOPMENT ACTIVITIES

Organisation & Planning:
Actively involved in the development, management and activities associated with the Civil Engineering Faculty Social Club, Engineering Undergraduates' Association and University Sailing Club in which I gained much from holding such offices as Secretary, President and Member of Committees

Leadership & Physical Fitness:
Corporal Australian Army Reserve (University Regiment / Construction Regiment) March 1992 to present. My continuing interest in this activity is reflected in the Officer Training I am currently undertaking

USEFUL PRACTICAL EXPERIENCE

Engineering: Training Program, Department of Marine and Harbours, Design, Maintenance & Inspection Branches - 3 months
Traffic Surveyor, Sinclair Knight (Consulting Engineers) - 4 months

Other: Night Order Manager, Coles New World, supervision of 25 staff - 4 months
Factory Hand, Cool Air Pty Ltd (Air Conditioning Components Manufacture) - 2 months
Factory Hand, Bevans Screen Printers - 2 months

OTHER FACTS

Born 21 September 1974 ... experienced in PC computer usage including design and graphics software ... completed secondary education at Adelaide Technical High with HSC Aggregate 359 (earned Engineering Science Prize Year 12) ... selected for Opportunity School placement during primary education

Referees will be provided on request

GEORGINA MILLS

<u>35 Jarrah Road, Henderson 6166</u>   <u>Tel: 08 9518 1936</u>

CAREER OBJECTIVE:
To apply my learning and practical experiences in Information Management and Librarianship to the data management, search and retrieval activities for user needs within a commercial, industrial, legal or medical employment environment. An opportunity to utilise my training in Psychology, Data Processing and Statistics would be an additional pleasure.

TERTIARY EDUCATION ACHIEVEMENTS:
- Diploma in Information Management-Librarianship graduating November 1997 from Curtin University of Technology
- BA Major: Psychology including Research Methods and Statistics completed at University of Western Australia 1996 Achieved Distinction and several Credits and gained much from Health and Business Management subjects

FORMAL STUDY HIGHLIGHTS:
- Achieving Distinctions and Credits in Information Management studies
- Award for Academic Excellence by Fellows of Blaxland College, University of Western Australia
- Developing personal independence by living at residential college and actively contributing to committee work for a variety of endeavours

COMPETENCIES AND CHARACTER:

Software Familiarity:	SIR	SPSSX (Stats)
	STAIRS	BASE
On-line Database Usage:	DIALOG	CLIRS
	MEDLINE	

Systems: Library Automated Processing/Cataloguing
Personal: Good team member
Clear written and oral skills
Effective planner used to providing service to public

WORK AND LEARNING EXPERIENCES:
- Retail Sales at Myers
- Circuit Board manufacture at Electronic Industries
- Office tasks within a Doctor's Practice, at Reading and Learning and the Arthritis Foundation of Australia
- Checkout Operator at Clancy's
- Tutoring in Psychology, Sociology, Biomathematics and Education

PEOPLE WHO KNOW ME WELL:
- Dr J Smithfield, College Master, University of Western Australia Tel: 08 9723 2679
- Mr J W Phillips, Managing Director, Phillips Industries Tel: 08 9372 1733
- Ms R Suitor, Managing Director, Suitor & Associates Tel: 08 9836 2911

OTHER FACTS ABOUT ME:
Born 16 November 1975...enjoy ocean yacht sailing...travel experiences include Europe, South East Asia and South Pacific... completed secondary education at St Margaret's College with HSC ranking of Top 15% of WA...prepared to relocate subject to nature of career opportunity

KYLIE BURNS

Tel: (08) 8372 1675 (Home)

CAREER OBJECTIVE

To be successful in the Human Care field, that is, to become aware of other people's needs and helping to provide them

EDUCATIONAL ACHIEVEMENTS

- Have completed and passed a six week Dining Room Service course at School of Hospitality and Tourism, Adelaide College of TAFE
- Obtained the Higher School Certificate at Brighton High School in 1996

USEFUL WORKING EXPERIENCES

- Dealing with the general public features in my current part-time employment at Adelaide Arts Centre
- Completed a five-day work experience program in the Social Work Department at the Royal Adelaide Hospital (June 1994)
- Voluntary school canteen assistant, 1995-96
- Worked as a full-time Dental Assistant (2 months, Jan-Mar 1997) where I learned about general accountancy, cleanliness and loyalty
- Baby-sitting on a regular basis. This developed my awareness of responsibility, thus maturity

PERSONAL DEVELOPMENT ACTIVITIES

- Have been actively involved in the 48 Hour Famine and the M.S. Read-A-Thon over a period of two years. Also collected donations for the Red Cross
- Bronze Star (Life Saving), 1992
- School Choir, 1992
- Helped organise and then participated in two fashion parades held for the general public (1993-94)
- Represented the school at grade level in basketball (1992-93) and volleyball (1995)
- Been active in Brownies and Guides (1987-93); learnt many different practical skills through camping, working at interest badges and weekly meetings

PERSONAL INFORMATION

- Date of Birth: 14 January 1979
- Address: 31 Prince Albert Street, Brighton, 5048
- Enjoy the outdoors and am currently pursuing my interest in the Japanese language; enjoy challenges and believe I am a fast learner

REFERENCES WILL BE PROVIDED ON REQUEST

Résumé of:

COLIN SCHELL

82 Liverpool Street, Kenwick 6107
Tel: (H) 08 9283 7298

OBJECTIVE

To apply my technical knowledge diligently acquired through formal studies and enthusiasm for my career path choice to employment tasks associated with Film Production with a particular preference for involvement in Video making.

FORMAL TRAINING ACHIEVEMENTS

- Visual Concepts College (VCC). Graduated in July 1997 following twelve months intensive formal training.
  Syllabus of studies completed attached as a photocopy

- Murdoch University. Completed several subjects successfully, including Computing, Mathematics and Statistics within the Bachelor of Arts program before electing to change direction of studies

SIGNIFICANT PERSONAL ACHIEVEMENTS

- Achieved 89% results in examinations at VCC and 'Excellent' gradings over two semesters
- Special Award for Attendance and Conscientiousness (VCC)
- Nominated as Best Camera Operator and for Best All-round student

EQUIPMENT FAMILIARITY

Video Editing (U-Matic Off-line)
Lighting (Blondies, Redheads, Arrie Lights)
Video Cameras (Sony M3, Sony Trinicon)
Video Production Logistics and Equipment for Studio and Location filming (Interiors and Outdoors)

USEFUL EMPLOYMENT LEARNING EXPERIENCES

- Security responsibilities for Student Union, Murdoch University
- Earned Licence and subsequent employed as Taxi Driver
- Miscellaneous learning situations while studying also include baby-sitting, boat cleaning and corporate video making

Colin Schell   **Page 2**

PEOPLE WHO KNOW ME WELL

"Colin has shown a marked ability in most subjects in the Film and Television course and particularly in practical aspects such as camera work, lighting, editing and technical operations..."

Extract from letter available for perusal from
Jonathon Mackay, Coordinator,
Visual Concepts College

PERSONAL

Born 15 July 1977...have a versatile attitude to initial employment tasks...main quest is employment within my chosen career and industry...prepared to continue formal studies subject to discussions with my employer...prepared to relocate ...not adverse to travel or shift work or assignment to remote locations...enjoy a range of athletic pursuits...handle tense situations well.

10 Sample Letters for Students

In your job application letter, your aim is to make the employer want to meet you. For this to happen, your letter has to be better than those of most of the other applicants.

The following sample letters will help you write a good job application letter of your own. Read all of them carefully. Again, as with the sample résumés, the aims of the people writing these letters will differ from your own and they may well mention things you have not done. These letters will, nonetheless, be able to give you a good, general idea. Underline or highlight sentences that you might be able to use or change to suit your situation. You should obtain good results by constructing your letters in similar ways to the samples.

Easy-to-Find Index

Sample Letters for Students

Checklists and Other Help for Your Letters

When you have prepared the first draft of your letter, refer to the following checklists to ensure you have put together all the information in the best possible format:

Application for Apprenticeship

> I am seeking an Electrical Trade apprenticeship with your organisation. My preference is for a Trainee Apprenticeship rather than an Indentured Apprenticeship.
>
> A résumé is enclosed which highlights the practical experience I have acquired with qualified electricians and my availability for employment at the conclusion of my HSC studies in November 1997.
>
> A message about an interview appointment can be telephoned to (08) 9257 1593.

Application for Part-Time Employment

> On those occasions when you are short of staff, your business could gain from my skills and willingness to work hard. This could be achieved without the cost to you of a full-time employee.
>
> Services that I am eager to provide are manuscript reviews and appraisals, copy drafting, proofreading, research, indexing and general office tasks. My qualifications include a completed Arts degree from Monash University (majoring in English Literature and Language), three-quarters of a Law degree and current honours work in Political Science. These studies have given me valuable experience in the use of English, an appreciation of style and composition, as well as skills in footnoting and indexing. I can honestly say that I have enjoyed this work.
>
> In readiness for my approach to you, I have purchased and familiarised myself with the Style Manual for Authors, Editors and Printers (AGPS publication).
>
> My university attendance requirements for the next nine months are only four hours a week, which means I am available during most business hours.
>
> I am eager to undertake any tasks assigned to me, both within and outside business hours.
>
> Please call me to arrange an opportunity to meet.

Application for Cadetship

I would like to be considered for a Cadetship with your organisation. My tertiary education commences next month at the University of Western Australia, where I have been accepted by the Faculty of Engineering.

Mechanical projects have interested me for the past five years. Last year my school careers adviser arranged a work experience program for me with a local firm. For two weeks I worked in a large automotive workshop and this strengthened my interest in mechanical engineering.

Part-time employment in a garage helped me save sufficient money to buy an old car, which I have subsequently learnt to dismantle and reassemble.

I am writing to you because I have heard good reports about your training and the interest your firm takes in its employees. Reference material in our careers library at school has provided me with more information about your firm.

A summary of further information about me is enclosed. A message to arrange an interview with you may be left on 9831.9452 (home).

Vacation Employment Application

My objective is to obtain employment with you for the period December to February. I am currently a full-time student in Business Studies at the University of South Australia. In June next year I expect to graduate with a Bachelor of Business degree, majoring in Operations Management.

To supplement my studies, I have obtained regular casual work in a retail menswear store. From this experience I have gained some awareness of current business trends and of serving the public.

The vacation employment positions you have advertised appear to offer the scope for further practical work experience I know that I need. Employment with you would have the benefit of testing my aptitude for my first preference for a career and relating my studies to the practical world of work.

Please contact me or leave a message on 9344 3916.

Letter Prior to Campus Interview

I was delighted to learn that your company will be recruiting at the business school, here at Charles Sturt University (Mitchell campus). As one of the December graduates, I'm immediately available for employment following graduation.

I have a strong Marketing background, enhanced by extensive activities with the school's Marketing Club and useful work experience during vacations.

I'm enclosing my résumé for your perusal prior to your visit and very much look forward to our personal meeting on 22 October—I'm the first person on your schedule that morning.

Application for Management Trainee

Position as Marketing Trainee — Publishing

I wish to be considered as a candidate for your recently advertised position for a Marketing Trainee. I am keen to combine my marketing skills with my literary interest to launch a career in the Publishing industry.

As well as a Marketing Degree from Griffith University, I have 2 1/2 years of commercial experience with CSR Limited, of which two years involved market, industry and product assessments for use by Divisional General Management.

Publishing and books have always held a passion for me. I was Editor of my official school magazine, as well as a regular reporter for the school newsletter; Editor of the Richlands Hockey Club newsletter and a regular contributor to newspapers on behalf of the Club.

I am eager to learn more of the challenges of the position. Please contact me to arrange an appointment.

Acceptance of Employment Offer

I am happy to learn that Whist and Ace wants me as an Accounting Trainee. I see this as an excellent opportunity and accept the offer.

I will be relocating to Sydney, as requested, by 25 January to commence your orientation program for new employees.

Thank you again.

Response to Advertisements

> Your advertisement in *Graduate Outlook* has encouraged me to send my résumé for your review. I am keen to be considered for a position within your personnel department.
>
> The high standard of your firm and its position of leadership in the industry are known to me through my personal research and my acquaintance with two of your employees, Mike Smith and Joanne Carruthers.
>
> As Secretary of the School Social Committee and Chairman of the Drama Club, I learnt to appreciate the necessity of irregular working hours, retaining information confidentially, exercising my own judgement, as well as communicating effectively and maintaining good relationships with others.
>
> Holiday jobs have helped me to learn about work situations and have provided a practical insight into business problems.
>
> Please contact me about an interview by telephoning 5481 3920.

Response to Advertisements

> I would like to apply for the full-time position advertised by your company as a Display Trainee in the Fashion Department. Having nearly completed the Retail Training course at Sydney College of TAFE, I now feel prepared to take on the duties of such a position.
>
> Earlier I completed a two-year Fashion Technology course at East Sydney TAFE. This gave me the necessary skills to be able to assess many aspects of garment assembly.
>
> My enclosed résumé shows details of the subjects studied, plus evidence of other preparation for employment.
>
> Please contact me on 9906.9371. I am at home after 3.30 pm following my classes at TAFE.

Thankyou Letter to Referees

> In your conversation with Mary Keating of J P Norman Pty Ltd, you must really have sung my praises. She told me that she wished that every prospective employee could come so warmly recommended.
>
> Thanks to your help, the job is mine and I am to begin next Monday.

Unsolicited Application to Companies

I am interested in applying for a position with your store as a Sales Assistant. Preferably, I would like to work in the sports or electronic goods department, as I have had experience with these types of products. If there are no vacancies in these sections, however, I am confident that I would work just as well in another department.

I am near the completion of a merchandising course and feel confident I will be an effective sales assistant.

Would you please telephone me on 9430.3742 to arrange an interview at any time?

Unsolicited Application to Companies

My purpose in writing to you is to enquire about full-time positions you may have available. I have just completed an apprenticeship as an Electrical Fitter Mechanic at Harringtons, South Melbourne. Through my own research I have found your company to be of a high standard and reputation.

If a vacancy should occur over the next three months in the electrical trades, I would like to be considered.

My enclosed résumé briefly outlines the activities from which I have learnt the meaning of hard work and developed my attitude towards working conscientiously for my employer.

Follow-Up after Interview

This note is to thank you for your courtesy in granting me an interview yesterday for the position of Manufacturing Trainee.

I am very interested in this position and feel confident that my motivation and studies will help me to perform competently the duties which you described. I feel particularly qualified to handle the part-time studies at the same time as following your job rotation plan through the Manufacturing Division.

Your interest and consideration are really appreciated and I am eager to learn of your decision.

11 Web Sites for Job Seekers

Useful Internet Addresses (Web Sites)

We have assembled the following list of web sites which may assist you in your job search activities. While all were online at time of publication we cannot guarantee their ongoing existence nor the quality of their assistance. Happy searching!

http://www.

Information about content of occupations

Aussie Careers Guide
northnet.com.au/~achamber

Careers OnLine
careersonline.com.au

Job Guide
jobguide.deet.gov.au/JobGuideOnline/

Course information

TAFE NSW Career Launch Site
tafensw.edu.au

OZJAC
curriculum.edu.au

Labour market information

Australian Bureau of Statistics (Labour Force Data)
abs.gov.au

Finding a career counsellor / job hunt adviser

Australian Association of Career Counsellors (AACC)
adelaide.net.au/~aacc

Worklife—The Centre for Worklife Counselling
ozemail.com.au/~worklife

Career Counsellors
jobplace@jobweb.com.au

Career transition help publications

Worklife—The Centre for Worklife Counselling
ozemail.com.au/~worklife

New Hobsons Press
camrev.com.au/nhp/index.html

Applying for jobs

JobWeb Australia
jobweb.com.au/career

What Color Is Your Parachute (Richard Nelson Bolles) site
washingtonpost.com/parachute

Interview rehearsal training

Worklife—The Centre for Worklife Counselling
ozemail.com.au/~worklife

Careers OnLine: Job seeker's workshop, careers show
careersonline.com.au

Posting your résumé on the www

Aust Resume Server
herenow.com.au/mhn_link.html

Professionals On Line
wordsimages.com/

JobWeb Australia
jobweb.com.au/postares.htm

Vacancy information

AK Jobnet, Austin Knight Company
ak.com.au/

Armstrong's Recruitment Advertising
armstrongs.com.au/

Byron employment australia
byron.com.au

Contractors Direct (IT Professionals)
ozemail.com.au/~itheads/

Employment Opportunities Australia
employment.com.au/ (also leads to Career Mosaic)

Enter Artsmedia (multimedia vacancies)
artsmedia.com.au

Fairfax Market
fairfax.com.au/jobs/mkt/html

gradlink™ (Graduate Careers Council of Australia)
  gradlink.edu.au

Job Network
  jobsearch.deetya.gov.au/

Job Web Australia
  jobweb.com.au/

Monster Board Australia
  monsterboard.com.au/

Morgan & Banks Job Search Site 'The Job Hound'
  morganbanks.com.au

News Limited
  newsclassifieds.com.au

PeopleSearch International
  peoplesearch.com.au

Phoenix (IT industry)
  phoenix.com.au

Web Wombat (links to employment consultants)
  webwombat.com.au

12 Choosing the Right Career Transition Coach

Becoming a wise consumer of career advisory services can not only assist the resolution of your current worklife issue but also increase your personal career self-resiliency for coping better with future career events—both expected and unexpected. The following will help you secure appropriate services at an affordable price. The best time to consider such services is before you really need them! Looking at your career situation while you have a job often provides a more thorough reasoned and planning process than if your situation has reached the urgent phase.

Cost

The cost of career services is important but should not be your only consideration. Cost should be weighed along side other factors such as the relevance of the service to your needs and the providers' credentials. It is quite rare for a client's issue to be resolved in one meeting. Be prepared for the likelihood of meeting more than once until you have all the right help you need. Be cautious of packaged fee arrangements. The preferred way of engaging skilled career support help is by way of an hourly charge. In this situation you pay as you go and re-hire your adviser as and when you need to and can afford to.

Career Advisers

These can be titled career counsellors, worklife coaches, personal career trainers, or even life management facilitators. The career services provider may be a firm with one of these or a team, some with specialisation in different aspects of career support help. In Australia it is useful to enquire whether they are registered members of the Australian Association of Career Counsellors as this indicates that their service is governed by a code of professional conduct and that they receive regular updates on professional practice techniques.

Workshops

Some career services offer a range of workshops relating to career planning, résumé writing, interview rehearsals. You need to decide whether you would prefer to work in a small group or within the privacy of a one-to-one relationship with the career adviser you engage.

Testing

Many modern day career advisers do not use psychological tests. This does not mean that such tests are not helpful but that the use of career self-assessment instruments are their preferred way of assisting your self-exploration and career transition.

Job Placement

Almost all career advisers do not place you in jobs. Their purpose is to empower you to find one yourself. Nevertheless they should have a thorough knowledge of the local labour market and be able to guide you to the more fruitful directions.

Other Services

Are you seeking computer assisted career planning? or access to the most relevant recommended Internet Web sites for your purpose? Are you seeking information about interstate job seeking or overseas? Do you want advice on scannable electronic resumes? Would you like access to a career library for your research?

Your Preparation

Make sure you define what you believe you need and ask for details about the services. It helps if you write down the issue you want to resolve. This can be faxed or emailed to your prospective helper or brought to your first meeting. When you have defined your problem it is easier to enquire:

- how would you help me?
- what is the prediction of costs I would incur?
- how long have you been helping people?
- do I have to sign a contract?

The above has been assisted by advice from The Center for Life Decisions and *What Color is Your Parachute?* (R. Nelson Bolles)

The Worklife Network (Established in 1979)

The term 'worklife' was chosen to reflect our continuing work in research, counselling, training and publishing material which relates to improving people's enjoyment from their employment activities and other aspects of their lives.

We do not accept the traditional view of career support—that is, to help people acquire satisfaction only from their working hours. We consider that occupational satisfaction can only occur when a person's total needs are included in the assessment of what is lacking and what needs to be done to increase inner well-being, improved relationships with others, and effective performance both at work and non-work activities. 'Life' in Worklife means our focus is on the total person. 'Work' relates to the roles in which the person is involved (employee, student, home-carer, and citizen) and their environments (workplace, educational institution, home, community).

Ours is a holistic approach—in our counselling and career training workshops we consider all features of a person at the same time as maintaining respect for personal privacy by use of non-threatening inquiries into thoughts and circumstances.

Worklife has representatives throughout Australia and New Zealand as well as in USA, Sweden, Norway and South Africa.

Career Transition Help

Worklife's career experts provide coaching help with:
- Job goal targeting
- Making decisions between options
- Interview rehearsals
- Finding the 'hidden' employment market
- Negotiation techniques
- Managing interactions with employment agencies
- Obtaining a job overseas or interstate
- On the job career strategies

Tel: (02) 9968 1588
Web Site: www.ozemail.com.au/~worklife